THE ULTIMATE
LOW FAT BAKING
COOKBOOK

THE ULTIMATE
$\mathcal{L}$OW$\mathcal{F}$AT$\mathcal{B}$AKING
COOKBOOK

The best-ever step-by-step collection of low fat baking recipes for
tempting and healthy eating

Consultant Editor: Linda Fraser

HERMES
HOUSE

This edition is published by Hermes House,
an imprint of Anness Publishing Ltd,
108 Great Russell Street, London WC1B 3NA;
info@anness.com

www.hermeshouse.com; www.annesspublishing.com

If you like the images in this book and would
like to investigate using them for publishing,
promotions or advertising, please visit our website
www.practicalpictures.com for more information.

A CIP catalogue record for this book is available
from the British Library.

Publisher: Joanna Lorenz
Senior Editor: Cathy Marriott
Designer: Lilian Lindblom
Illustrations: Anna Koska

NOTES

Bracketed terms are intended for American readers.
For all recipes, quantities are given in both metric
and imperial measures and, where appropriate,
in standard cups and spoons. Follow one set of
measures, but not a mixture, because they are
not interchangeable.
Standard spoon and cup measures are level.
1 tsp = 5ml, 1 tbsp = 15ml, 1 cup = 250ml/8fl oz.
Australian standard tablespoons are 20ml.
Australian readers should use 3 tsp in place of
1 tbsp for measuring small quantities.
American pints are 16fl oz/2 cups. American readers
should use 20fl oz/2.5 cups in place of 1 pint when
measuring liquids.
Electric oven temperatures in this book are for
conventional ovens. When using a fan oven, the
temperature will probably need to be reduced by
about 10–20°C/20–40°F. Since ovens vary, you
should check with your manufacturer's instruction
book for guidance.
The nutritional analysis given for each recipe is
calculated per portion (i.e. serving or item), unless
otherwise stated. If the recipe gives a range, such as
Serves 4–6, then the nutritional analysis will be for
the smaller portion size, i.e. 6 servings. The analysis
does not include optional ingredients, such as salt
added to taste.
Medium (US large) eggs are used unless
otherwise stated.

PUBLISHER'S NOTE

Although the advice and information in this book
are believed to be accurate and true at the time
of going to press, neither the authors nor the
publisher can accept any legal responsibility or
liability for any errors or omissions that may have
been made nor for any inaccuracies nor for any
loss, harm or injury that comes about from
following instructions or advice in this book.

Contents

Introduction

When we talk of cakes and baking we tend to imagine rich, calorie-laden treats that are well out of reach if you are following a low-fat diet. With reduced-fat cooking methods, however, it is very easy to create delicious, low-fat desserts, cakes and bakes that are also full of flavour and appeal. It is generally agreed that a high-fat diet is bad for us, especially if the fats are of the saturated variety. Unless you are making meringues or angel cakes, it is rarely possible to do entirely without fat in baking. Nevertheless, it is possible to cut down considerably on the amount used, and equally good results can be achieved using healthier unsaturated oils instead of saturated fats.

Polyunsaturated oils such as sunflower oil, corn oil and safflower oil are excellent for most baking purposes, but choose olive oil which is mono-unsaturated for recipes that require a good, strong flavour. When an oil is not suitable, a soft margarine which is high in polyunsaturates is the fat to choose. Low-fat spreads are ideal for spreading but not good for baking, as they contain a high proportion of water.

Although cheese is high in saturated fat, its flavour makes it invaluable in many recipes. Choose either reduced-fat or half-fat varieties with a mature flavour, or a lesser amount of a highly flavoured cheese such as Parmesan. When using less fat, you can add extra moisture to cakes and teabreads in the form of fresh or dried fruits. There is no need to use full cream (whole) milk – try skimmed milk or fruit juice instead. Buttermilk (the liquid left over from churning butter) is, surprisingly, virtually fat free and is perfect for soda bread and scones. Cream undoubtedly adds a touch of luxury to special occasion cakes, however, fromage frais, thick yogurt or curd cheese sweetened with honey make delicious low-fat fillings and toppings for even the most elaborate cakes.

So, you will see that using less fat doesn't prevent you from making scrumptious cakes and bakes that look and taste every bit as good as those made traditionally with butter and cream. The recipes in this book are sure to inspire, impress and amaze everyone who believed low-fat baking to be an idea too good to be true.

Left: Everyone loves fresh breads, scones and biscuits straight from the oven.

Store Cupboard

Cutting down on fat doesn't mean sacrificing taste. Instead, choose basic ingredients that are naturally lower in fat. This is not so limiting as it sounds, as the following ingredients show.

FLOURS

Mass-produced, highly refined flours are fine for most baking purposes, but for the very best results choose organic stone-ground flours because they will add flavour as well as texture to your baking.

Rye flour

This dark-coloured flour has a low gluten content and gives a dense loaf with a good flavour. It is best mixed with strong wheat flour to give a lighter loaf.

Soft flour

This flour, sometimes called sponge flour, contains less gluten than plain flour and is ideal for light cakes and biscuits.

Strong (bread) flour

Made from hard wheat which contains a high proportion of gluten, this flour is the one to use for bread-making.

Wholemeal (whole-wheat) flour

Because this flour contains the complete wheat kernel, it gives a coarser texture and a good wholesome flavour to bread.

NUTS AND SEEDS

Most nuts are low in saturated fats and high in polyunsaturated fats. Use them sparingly as their total fat content is high. Sunflower seeds, poppy and linseeds are good for decorating rolls or adding texture.

YEAST

Dried yeast helps bread to rise.

HERBS AND SPICES

Chopped fresh herbs add a great deal of interest to baking. They add flavour to breads, scones and soda breads. In the absence of fresh herbs, dried herbs can be used: less is needed but the flavour is generally not as good.

Spices can add either strong or subtle flavours depending on the amount used. Ground cinnamon, nutmeg and mixed spice are most useful for baking but more exotic spices, such as saffron or cardamom, can also be used to great effect.

Buy herbs and spices from a shop with a high turnover to ensure optimum freshness and flavour.

SWEETENERS

Dried fruits

These are a traditional addition to cakes and teabreads. There is a wide range available, including more unusual varieties such as peach, pineapple, banana and mango, as well as more familiar currants and glacé (candied) cherries. Natural sugars in dried fruits add sweetness to baked goods and keep them moist, making it possible to use less fat.

Fruit juice

Concentrated fruit juices are very useful for baking. They have no added sweeteners or preservatives and can be diluted as required. Use them in their concentrated form for baking or for sweetening fillings.

Honey

Good honey has a strong flavour so you can use rather less of it than the equivalent amount of sugar. It also contains traces of minerals and vitamins.

Malt extract

This is a sugary by-product of barley. It has a strong flavour and is ideal for bread, cakes and teabreads as it adds moisture.

Molasses

This is the residue left after the first stage of refining sugar cane. It has a strong, smoky and slightly bitter taste that gives a good flavour to bakes and cakes. Black treacle can often be used as a substitute for molasses.

Pear and apple or other fruit spreads

This is a very concentrated fruit juice with no added sugar. It has a sweet–sour taste and can be used as a spread or blended with a little fruit juice and added to baking recipes as a sweetener.

Unrefined sugars

Most baking recipes call for sugar; choose unrefined sugars rather than refined sugars, as they have more flavour and contain some minerals.

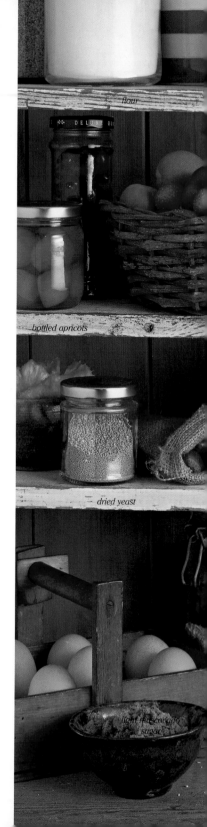

flour

bottled apricots

dried yeast

light muscovado sugar

Right: It's easier to follow a healthy eating plan if you have a store cupboard full of tempting ingredients that are naturally low in fat.

currants   poppy seeds   honey   herbs

fresh fruit   oatmeal   cinnamon sticks   dried apricots   sesame seeds

sunflower seeds

physalis

linseed

raisins   glacé cherries   olive oil   extra virgin olive oil   pear and apple spread   apricot compôte   dates

fresh fruit

rolled oats

blueberries

orange juice

Oils, Fats and Dairy Produce

LOW-FAT OILS AND FATS

Low-fat spreads are ideal for spreading on breads and teabreads, but are unfortunately not suitable for baking because they have a high water content.

When you are baking, try to avoid saturated fats such as butter and hard margarine and use oils high in polyunsaturates such as sunflower, corn or safflower oil. When margarine is essential, choose a variety that is high in polyunsaturates.

Low-fat spread, rich buttermilk blend
Made with a high proportion of buttermilk, which is naturally low in fat. Unsuitable for baking.

Olive oil
Use this mono-unsaturated oil when a recipe requires a good strong flavour. It is best to use extra virgin olive oil.

Olive oil reduced-fat spread
Based on olive oil, this spread has a better flavour than some other low-fat spreads, but is not suitable for baking.

Reduced-fat butter
This contains about 40% fat; the rest is water and milk solids emulsified together. It is not suitable for baking.

Sunflower light
Not suitable for baking as it contains only 40% fat, plus emulsified water and milk solids.

Sunflower oil
High in polyunsaturates, this is the oil used most frequently in this book as it has a pleasant but not too dominant flavour.

Very low-fat spread
Contains only 20–30% fat and so is not suitable for baking.

LOW-FAT CHEESES

There are many low-fat cheeses that can be used in baking. Generally, harder cheeses have a higher fat content than soft cheeses. Choose mature (sharp) cheese whenever possible as you need less of it to give a good flavour.

Cottage cheese
A low-fat soft cheese that is also available in a half-fat form.

Curd (farmers') cheese
This is a low-fat soft cheese made with either skimmed or semi-skimmed milk and can be used instead of cream cheese.

Edam and Maasdam
Two medium-fat hard cheeses well suited to baking.

Feta cheese
This is a medium-fat cheese with a firm, crumbly texture. It has a slightly sour, salty flavour which can range from rather bland to strong.

Half-fat Cheddar and Red Leicester
These contain about 14% fat.

Mozzarella light
This is a medium-fat version of an Italian soft cheese.

Quark
Made from fermented skimmed milk, this soft, white cheese is virtually free of fat.

CREAM ALTERNATIVES

Yogurt and fromage frais make excellent alternatives to cream, and when combined with honey, liqueurs or other flavourings they make delicious fillings or toppings for cakes and bakes.

Bio yogurt
This contains friendly bacterial cultures that aid digestion. Bio yogurt has a mild, sweet taste.

Crème fraîche
This thick soured cream has a mild, lemony taste. Look out for half-fat crème fraîche which has a fat content of 15%.

Fromage frais
This is a soft cheese available in two grades: virtually fat free (0.4% fat), and a more creamy variety (7.9% fat).

Greek (US strained plain) yogurt
This thick, creamy yogurt is made from whole milk with a fat content of 10%. A low-fat version is also available.

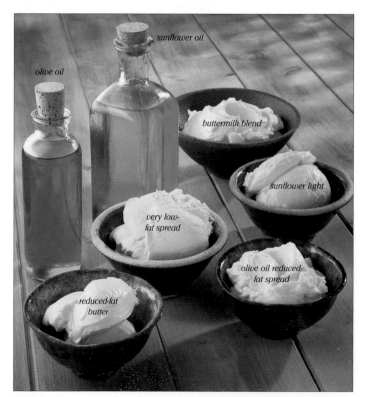

sunflower oil

olive oil

buttermilk blend

sunflower light

very low-fat spread

olive oil reduced-fat spread

reduced-fat butter

Left: Try to avoid using saturated fats such as butter and margarine. Instead use oils or spreads high in polyunsaturates.

curd cheese

Mozzarella

cottage cheese

Edam

Maasdam

Cheddar

feta

Red Leicester

soft cheese

quark

semi-skimmed milk

buttermilk

low-fat yogurt

half-fat crème fraîche

bio yogurt

eggs

light fromage frais

Above: There are a whole range of lower-fat cheeses that can be used in baking.

Left: Use low-fat milks for baking and try yogurt or fromage frais as an alternative to cream.

LOW-FAT MILKS

Buttermilk

Made from skimmed milk with a bacterial culture added, it is very low in fat.

Powdered skimmed milk

A useful, low-fat standby.

Semi-skimmed milk

With a fat content of only 1.5–1.8%, this milk tastes less rich than full-cream milk. It is favoured by many people for everyday use for precisely this reason.

Skimmed milk

This milk has had virtually all the fat removed leaving only 0.1–0.3%. It is ideal for those wishing to cut down their fat intake.

EGGS

These are essential for baking.

Equipment

If you choose good quality, heavy non-stick cookware, the amount of fat used in baking can be kept to an absolute minimum.

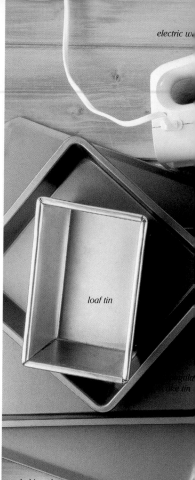

electric w...

loaf tin

Baking parchment
For lining tins and baking sheets to ensure cakes, meringues and biscuits do not stick.

Baking sheet
Choose a large, heavy baking sheet that will not warp at high temperatures.

Balloon whisk
Perfect for whisking egg whites and incorporating air into other light mixtures.

Box grater
This multi-purpose grater can be used for citrus rind, fruit and vegetables, and cheese.

Brown paper
Used for wrapping around the outside of cake tins (pans) to protect the cake mixture from the full heat of the oven.

Cake tester
A simple implement that, when inserted into a cooked cake, will come out clean if the cake is ready.

Cook's knife
This has a heavy, wide blade and is ideal for chopping.

Deep round cake tin (pan)
This deep tin is ideal for baking fruit cakes.

Electric whisk
Ideal for creaming cake mixtures, whipping cream and whisking egg whites.

Honey twirl
For spooning honey without making a mess!

Juicer
Made from porcelain, glass or plastic – used for squeezing the juice from citrus fruits.

Loaf tin (pan)
Available in various sizes and used for making loaf-shaped breads and teabreads.

Measuring jug (cup)
Absolutely essential for measuring any kind of liquid accurately.

Measuring spoons
Standard measuring spoons are essential for measuring small quantities of ingredients.

Mixing bowls
A set of different sized bowls is essential in any kitchen for whisking and mixing.

Muffin tin (pan)
Shaped into individual cups, this tin is much simpler to use than individual paper cases. It can also be used for baking small pies and tarts.

Nutmeg grater
This miniature grater is used for grating whole nutmegs.

Nylon sieve
Suitable for most baking purposes, and particularly for sieving foods that react adversely with metal.

Palette knife (metal spatula)
This implement is needed for loosening pies, tarts and breads from baking sheets and for smoothing icing over cakes.

Pastry brush
Useful for brushing excess flour from pastry and brushing glazes over pastries, breads and tarts.

Pastry (cookie) cutters
A variety of shapes and sizes of cutter is useful when stamping out pastry, biscuits and scones.

Rectangular cake tin (pan)
For making tray cakes and bakes, served cut into slices.

Ring mould
Perfect for making angel cakes and other ring-shaped cakes.

Sandwich cake tin (pan)
Ideal for sponge cakes; make sure you have two of them!

Scissors
Vital for cutting paper and snipping dough and pastry.

Square cake tin (pan)
Used for making square cakes or cakes served cut into smaller squares.

Swiss roll tin (jelly roll pan)
This shallow tin is designed especially for Swiss rolls.

Vegetable knife
A useful knife for preparing the fruit and vegetables that you may add to your bakes.

Wire rack
Ideal for cooling cakes and bakes, allowing the circulation of air, which will prevent sogginess.

Wire sieve
A large wire sieve is ideal for most normal baking purposes.

Wooden spoon
Essential for mixing ingredients and creaming mixtures.

baking sheet

balloon whisk

wooden spoon

cook's knife

Right: Invest in a few useful items for easy low-fat cooking: non-stick cookware and accurate measuring equipment are essential.

mixing bowls

baking
parchment

brown paper

scissors

sandwich
cake tin

ring mould

pastry brush

wire rack

measuring jug

deep round
cake tin

pastry
cutters

etable knife

honey
twirl

wire rack

Swiss roll tin

juicer

box grater

nutmeg
grater

wire sieve

nylon sieve

measuring
spoons

muffin tin

Facts about Fat

It's easy to cut down on obvious sources of fat such as butter, margarine, cream, whole milk and high-fat cheeses, but watch out for "hidden" fats.

Most of us eat more fat every day than the 10g/¼oz that our bodies need; on average we each consume about 115g/4oz fat each day. Current nutritional advice isn't quite that strict on fat intake though, and it suggests that we should limit our daily intake to no more than 30% of total calories. In real terms, this means that for an average intake of 2,000 calories a day, 30% of energy would come from about 600 calories. Since each gram of fat provides 9 calories, your total daily intake should be no more than 67g/2½oz fat.

Although we may think of cakes and biscuits as sweet foods, more calories come from their fat than from their sugar. Indeed, of the quarter of our fat intake that comes from non-meat sources, a fifth comes from dairy products and margarine and the rest from cakes, biscuits, pastries and other foods. The merits of low-fat baking are enormous, as you are able not only to cut down on your fat intake in general, but you also have control over

Above: Animal products such as lard, suet, butter and some margarines are major sources of saturated fats.

exactly how much fat and the type of fat you and the rest of your family consume on a daily basis.

Fats can be divided into two main categories – saturated and unsaturated. We are all well aware of the dangers of saturated fats in relation to blocking arteries and causing coronary heart disease. Much of the saturated fat we eat comes from animal sources – meat and dairy products such as suet, lard and butter – which are solid at room temperature. However, there are also some saturated fats of vegetable origin, notably coconut and palm oils. In addition, a number of margarines are "hydrogenated", a process that increases the proportion of saturated fat they contain. Such margarine should be avoided.

Left: Some oils, such as olive oil and rapeseed, are thought to help lower blood cholesterol.

The Fat and Calorie Contents of Food

This chart shows the weight of fat and the energy content of 110g/3½oz of various foods.

Unsaturated fats can be divided into two main types: mono-unsaturated and poly-unsaturated. Mono-unsaturated fats are found in various foods including olive oil, rapeseed oil and some nuts. These fats may actually lower blood cholesterol and this could explain why in Mediterranean countries, where olive oil is widely consumed, there is such a low incidence of heart disease.

The most familiar polyunsaturated fats are of vegetable or plant origin and include sunflower oil, corn oil, soya oil, walnut oil and many soft margarines. It was believed at one time that it was beneficial to switch to polyunsaturated fats as they may also help lower cholesterol. Today, however, most experts believe that it is more important to reduce the total intake of all kinds of fat.

Above: Vegetable and plant oils and some margarines are high in polyunsaturated fat.

FRUIT AND NUTS	Fat	Energy
Apples, eating	0.1g	47Kcals/197kJ
Avocados	19.5g	190Kcals/795kJ
Bananas	0.3g	95Kcals/397kJ
Dried mixed fruit	1.6g	227Kcals/950kJ
Grapefruit	0.1g	30Kcals/155kJ
Oranges	0.1g	37Kcals/155kJ
Peaches	0.1g	33Kcals/138kJ
Almonds	55.8g	612Kcals/2560kJ
Brazil nuts	68.2g	682Kcals/2853kJ
Peanut butter, smooth	53.7g	623Kcals/2606kJ
Pine nuts	68.6g	688Kcals/2878kJ

DAIRY PRODUCE, FATS AND OILS	Fat	Energy
Cream, double (heavy)	48.0g	449Kcals/1897kJ
Cream, single (light)	19.1g	198Kcals/828kJ
Cream, whipping	39.3g	373Kcals/1560kJ
Milk, skimmed	0.1g	33Kcals/130kJ
Milk, whole	3.9g	66Kcals/276kJ
Cheddar cheese	34.4g	412Kcals/1724kJ
Cheddar-type, reduced fat	15.0g	216Kcals/1092kJ
Cream cheese	47.4g	439Kcals/1837kJ
Brie	26.9g	319Kcals/1335kJ
Edam cheese	25.4g	333Kcals/1393kJ
Feta cheese	20.2g	250Kcals/1046kJ
Parmesan cheese	32.7g	452Kcals/1891kJ
Greek yogurt	9.1g	115Kcals/481kJ
Low-fat yogurt, natural	0.8g	56Kcals/234kJ
Butter	81.7g	737Kcals/308kJ
Lard	99.0g	891Kcals/3730kJ
Low-fat spread	40.5g	390Kcals/1632kJ
Margarine	81.6g	739Kcals/3092kJ
Coconut oil	99.9g	899Kcals/3761kJ
Corn oil	99.9g	899Kcals/3761kJ
Olive oil	99.9g	899Kcals/3761kJ
Safflower oil	99.9g	899Kcals/3761kJ
Eggs (whole)	10.9g	147Kcals/615kJ
Egg white	trace	36Kcals/150kJ
Egg yolk	30.5g	339Kcals/1418kJ

OTHER FOODS	Fat	Energy
Sugar	0	94Kcals/648kJ
Chocolate, milk	30.3g	529Kcals/2213kJ
Honey	0	88Kcals/1205kJ
Jam	0	61Kcals/1092kJ
Marmalade	0	61Kcals/1092kJ
Lemon curd	5.1g	283Kcals/1184kJ

Techniques

Baking is easy and satisfying, even if you're a beginner. Just follow the recipes, the tips and the step-by-step techniques and you will get perfect results every time.

1 For liquids measured in jugs: use a glass or plastic measuring jug (cup). Put the jug on a flat surface and pour in the liquid. Bend down and check that the liquid is exactly level with the marking on the jug, as specified in the recipe.

2 For measuring dry ingredients in a spoon: fill the spoon with the ingredient. Level the surface even with the brim of the spoon, using the straight edge of a knife.

3 For liquids measured in spoons: pour the liquid into the measuring spoon, to the brim, and then pour it into the mixing bowl.

4 For measuring flour in a cup or spoon: scoop the flour from the canister or bag in the measuring cup or spoon. Hold it over the canister or bag and level the surface.

5 For measuring butter: cut with a sharp knife and weigh, or cut off the specified amount following the markings on the wrapping paper.

6 For lining cake tins (pans): lightly grease the tin, then measure and cut pieces of baking parchment to fit the base and sides of the tin.

7 For muffin tins (pans): use paper cases of the required size or grease and flour the tins.

Using Yeast

There are three main types of yeast currently available – dried, easy-blend and fresh. Easy-blend is added directly to the dry ingredients, whereas dried and fresh yeast must first be mixed with warm liquid and a little sugar to activate them.

USING DRIED YEAST

1 Measure dried yeast, then sprinkle it into the warm liquid in a jug (pitcher) or small bowl with a pinch of sugar. Stir well and set aside in a warm place for about 10–15 minutes.

2 When the yeast liquid becomes frothy, stir into the dry ingredients.

Cook's Tip
Dried yeast doesn't dissolve well in milk. You must either leave it for about 30 minutes to froth, or if you are in a hurry, dissolve it in a little water first.

USING EASY-BLEND DRIED YEAST

1 Add easy-blend (rapid-rise) dried yeast to the dry ingredients directly from the packet. Do not dissolve it in liquid first.

USING FRESH YEAST

1 Place fresh yeast in a small bowl with a pinch of sugar and a little lukewarm water. Cream together until smooth, then leave for 5–10 minutes until frothy, before adding to the dry ingredients.

Making Muffins and Quick Breads

These bakes are fast and easy to make. The raising agent reacts quickly with moisture
and heat to make the muffins and breads rise, without the need for
a rising period before baking.

The raising agent is usually bicarbonate of soda (baking soda) or baking powder, which is a mixture of bicarbonate of soda and an acid salt such as cream of tartar. It will start to work as soon as it comes into contact with liquid, so don't mix the dry and liquid ingredients until just before you are ready to fill the muffin tins (pans) and bake them.

In addition to the thick-batter quick breads discussed here, there are also quick breads such as scones that are made from soft doughs.

Cook's Tip

Easy-blend (rapid-rise) is the most readily available dried yeast. Unlike ordinary dried yeast, there is no need to mix it with liquid. Just combine it with the flour and other dry ingredients and then add the warm liquids.

MUFFINS

1 Combine the dry ingredients in a bowl. It is a good idea to sift the flour with the raising agent, salt and any spices to mix them evenly. Add the liquid ingredients and stir just until the dry ingredients are moistened; the mixture will not be smooth. Do not overmix, attempting to remove all the lumps. If you do, the muffins will be tough and will have air holes in them.

2 Divide the mixture evenly among the greased muffin tins or deep bun tins (pans) lined with paper cases, filling them about two-thirds full. Bake until golden brown and a wooden skewer inserted in the centre comes out clean. To prevent soggy bottoms, remove the muffins immediately from the tins to a wire rack. Serve warm or cool to room temperature.

FRUIT AND/OR NUT TEABREADS

1 **Method 1:** stir together all the liquid ingredients. Add the dry ingredients and beat until smoothly blended.
Method 2: beat the butter with the sugar until the mixture is light and fluffy. Beat in the eggs followed by the other liquid ingredients. Stir in the dry ingredients. Pour the mixture into a prepared tin (pan) (typically a loaf tin). Bake until a wooden skewer inserted in the centre comes out clean. If the teabread is browning too quickly, cover the top with foil.

2 Cool in the tin for 5 minutes, then turn out on to a wire rack to cool completely. A lengthways crack on the surface is characteristic of teabreads. For easier slicing, wrap the bread in baking parchment and overwrap in foil, then store overnight at room temperature.

Making Breadsticks and Focaccia

Italian flatbreads such as focaccia and breadsticks can be topped with herbs and seeds for tasty accompaniments or starters.

Personalize breadsticks and focaccia with combinations of your favourite ingredients for unusual snacks, or split and fill flatbreads with ham or cheese for an Italian-style sandwich. This basic dough can be used for other recipes, such as pizza. The dough may be frozen before it is baked, and thawed before filling.

BREADSTICKS

1 There's no need for the first rising. Divide the dough into walnut-size pieces and roll out on a floured surface with your hands, into thin sausage shapes. Transfer to a greased baking sheet, cover and leave in a warm place for 10–15 minutes. Bake until crisp.

FOCACCIA

1 Warm a mixing bowl by swirling some hot water in it. Drain. Place the yeast in the bowl and pour on the warm water. Stir in the sugar, mix with a fork, and allow to stand for 5–10 minutes until the yeast has dissolved and starts to foam.

2 Use a wooden spoon to mix in the salt and about one-third of the flour. Mix in another third of the flour, stirring with the spoon until the dough forms a mass and begins to pull away from the sides of the bowl.

3 Sprinkle some of the remaining flour on to the smooth work surface. Remove the dough from the bowl and begin to knead it, working in the remaining flour a little at a time. Knead for 8–10 minutes. By the end the dough should be elastic and smooth. Form it into a ball.

4 Lightly oil a mixing bowl. Place the dough in the bowl. Stretch a damp tea towel or clear film (plastic wrap) across the top of the bowl, and leave it to stand in a warm place until the dough has doubled in volume, about 40–50 minutes or more, depending on the type of yeast used. To test whether the dough has risen enough, poke two fingers into the dough. If the indentations remain, the dough is ready to use.

5 Knock back (punch down) the dough with your fist to release the air. Knead for 1–2 minutes.

6 Brush a tin with oil. Press the dough into the tin with your fingers to a layer 2.5cm/1in thick. Cover and leave to rise for 30 minutes. Preheat the oven. Make indentations all over the focaccia with your fingers. Brush with oil, add filling and bake until pale golden brown.

Making Scones and Popovers

Scones are quick breads made with a soft dough based on flour and milk, with a raising agent added. Popovers are individual batter puddings, made in a similar way to Yorkshire puddings.

The dough for scones may be rolled out and cut into shapes, it may be dropped from a spoon on to a baking sheet, or lightly patted out and then stamped out with a cutter into rounds or other shapes.

SCONES

1 Sift together the dry ingredients into a large mixing bowl: flour, baking powder with or without bicarbonate of soda (baking soda), salt, sugar, spices etc.

2 Add the fat (butter, margarine or vegetable fat). With a pastry blender or two knives, cut the fat into the dry ingredients until the mixture resembles fine crumbs, or rub into the fat with your fingertips.

3 Add the liquid ingredients (milk, cream, buttermilk, eggs). Stir with a fork until the dry ingredients are thoroughly moistened and will come together in a ball of fairly soft dough in the centre of the bowl.

4 Turn the dough on to a lightly floured surface. Knead it very lightly, folding and pressing to mix evenly, for about 30 seconds. Roll or pat out the dough to a 2cm/¾in thickness.

5 With a floured, sharp-edged cutter, cut out rounds or other shapes. Arrange on an ungreased baking sheet. Brush with beaten egg or cream. Bake until golden brown. Serve immediately.

6 For griddle scones: if using a well-seasoned cast iron griddle, there is no need to grease it. Heat it slowly and evenly. Put scone triangles or rounds on the hot griddle and cook for 5–6 minutes on each side or until golden brown and cooked through.

POPOVERS

1 Sift the flour into a large bowl along with other dry ingredients such as salt and ground black pepper. Make a well in the centre of the dry ingredients and put in the eggs, egg yolks and some of the liquid.

2 With a wooden spoon, beat together the eggs and liquid in the well just to mix them. Gradually draw in some of the flour from the sides, stirring vigorously.

3 When the mixture is smooth, stir in the remaining liquid. Stir just until the ingredients are combined – the trick is not to overmix.

4 Pour the mixture into greased muffin tins (pans) or ramekins and bake until golden brown. Do not open the oven door during baking time or the popovers may collapse. Run a knife around the edge of each popover to loosen, then turn out and serve hot.

Cutting Tips for Scones

Be sure the cutter or knife is sharp so that the edges of the scone shapes are not compressed; this would prevent rising. Cut the shapes close together so that you won't have to re-roll the dough more than once. If necessary, a short, sturdy drinking glass can be pressed into service as a cutter. Flour the rim well and do not press too hard. When cutting out, don't twist the cutter.

Shaping Rolls

Bread rolls can be made in all kinds of interesting shapes and sizes. Begin by dividing the dough into even-size portions. Try these traditional variations first and then, when you are used to working with dough, experiment with your own customized designs.

1 To shape cottage rolls, divide each portion of dough into two, making one piece about twice the size of the other. Shape both pieces into smooth balls. Dampen the top of the large ball and place the small ball on top. Push a lightly floured index finger through the middle of the dough.

2 To shape clover leaf rolls, divide each portion of dough into three equal pieces. Form each piece into a smooth ball, lightly dampen, and arrange in a clover leaf formation. Lightly press together.

3 To shape knots, roll each dough portion into a fairly long sausage shape. Carefully knot the dough sausage, as you would a piece of string.

4 To shape braids, divide each dough portion into three equal pieces. Roll each piece into an even sausage shape. Dampen the three sausages at one end and pinch together. Braid the sausages loosely and pinch together at the other end, dampening lightly first.

5 To shape snipped-top rolls, roll each dough portion into a smooth ball. Using a pair of kitchen scissors, make two or three snips in the top of each ball.

6 To shape twists, divide each dough portion into two equal pieces. Roll each piece into an even sausage shape, then twist the two pieces together, dampening at each end and pressing together firmly.

Lining Baking Tins

Ensure that your cakes and teabreads don't stick by lining the tin with baking parchment.
Use low-fat margarine or oil to grease the tin lightly if necessary.

LINING A ROUND TIN

1 To line a round tin (pan), place the tin on baking parchment and draw around the edge. Cut out two circles that size, then cut a strip a little longer than the tin's circumference and one and a half times its depth. Lightly grease the tin and place one paper circle on the base. Make small diagonal cuts along one edge of the paper strip.

2 Put the paper strip inside the tin, with the snipped fringe along the base. Place the second paper circle in the base of the tin, covering the fringe. Grease once more.

LINING A SWISS ROLL TIN

1 To line a Swiss roll tin (jelly roll pan), cut a piece of baking parchment large enough to line the base and sides of the tin. Lay the paper over the tin and make four diagonal cuts, one from each corner of the paper to the nearest corner of the tin.

2 Lightly grease the tin. Place the paper in the tin and smooth into the sides, overlapping the paper corners to fit neatly.

LINING A LOAF TIN

1 To line a loaf tin (pan), measure and cut a strip of baking parchment to fit the depth and length of the tin.

2 Lightly grease the tin. Place the strip of paper in the tin so that the paper covers the base and comes up over both long sides. Then press the paper lining into place.

Testing Bread and Cakes

It is very important to check that cakes and bakes are properly cooked, otherwise they can be soggy and cakes may sink in the middle.

TESTING A FRUIT CAKE

1 To test if a fruit cake is ready, push a skewer or cake tester into it; the cake is cooked if the skewer or cake tester comes out clean.

2 Fruit cakes are generally left to cool in the tin for 30 minutes. When cool, turn the cake out carefully, peel away the paper and place on a wire rack or board.

TESTING A SPONGE CAKE

1 To test if a sponge cake is ready, press down lightly in the centre of the cake with your fingertips – if the cake springs back, it is cooked.

2 To remove the cooked sponge cake from the tin (pan), loosen around the edge by carefully scraping around the inside of the tin with a palette knife (metal spatula), invert the cake on to a wire rack, cover with a second rack, then invert again. Remove the top rack and leave to cool.

TESTING BREAD

1 To test if a loaf of bread is ready, first loosen the edges of the loaf with a palette knife (metal spatula), then tip out the loaf.

2 Hold the loaf upside down and tap it gently on the base. If it sounds hollow, the bread is cooked.

Icing a Cake

Confident icing of a cake makes all the difference to its appearance. With just a little practice, your cakes will look professional.

MAKING A PIPING BAG

Being able to make your own piping (pastry) bag is a very handy skill, particularly if you are dealing with small amounts of icing or several colours.

1 Fold a 25cm/10in square of baking parchment in half to form a triangle. Using the centre of the long side as the central tip, roll half the paper into a cone.

2 Holding the paper in position, continue to roll the other half of the triangle around the first, to form a complete cone.

3 Holding the cone firmly, fold the end of the paper triangle over the top into the inside of the cone to secure it. Fill the bag no more than half full with icing, fold over the top several times to seal, then snip off the tip to the required size.

ICING A CAKE

1 To create a simple zig-zag effect, ice the cake all over, then pipe lines in a different colour backwards and forwards over the top.

2 To create a feathered effect, follow step 1, then drag a knife through the icing at regular intervals in opposite directions, perpendicular to the lines.

3 To make a figure-of-eight, or a similar effect, ice the cake all over, then, using a different coloured icing, pipe figures of eight around the edge of the cake, in a steady stream.

Preparing Glazes and Citrus Fruits

Apricot glaze is extremely useful for brushing over any kind of fresh fruit topping or filling to give it a shiny appearance. Oranges, lemons and other citrus fruits are widely used in baking, both as flavouring and as decoration.

MAKING APRICOT GLAZE

1 Place a few spoonfuls of apricot jam in a small pan, with a squeeze of lemon juice. Heat the jam, stirring until it is melted and runny.

2 Pour the melted jam into a wire sieve set over a bowl. Stir the jam with a wooden spoon to help it go through.

3 Return the strained jam from the bowl to the pan. Keep the glaze warm and brush it generously over the fresh fruit until evenly coated.

PREPARING CITRUS FRUITS

1 To grate the rind from a citrus fruit, use the finest side of the grater. Don't remove any of the white pith and brush off any rind that remains in the grater.

2 To pare the rind from a citrus fruit, use a swivel vegetable peeler. Remove the rind in strips as if peeling a potato and don't remove any of the white pith.

3 To make citrus rind shreds, or julienne, cut strips of pared rind into very fine shreds using a sharp knife. Boil the shreds for a couple of minutes in water or sugar syrup to soften them.

Low-fat Whipped "Cream"

Serve this sweet "cream" instead of whipped double cream. It isn't suitable for cooking,
but freezes very well.

MAKING LOW-FAT WHIPPED "CREAM"

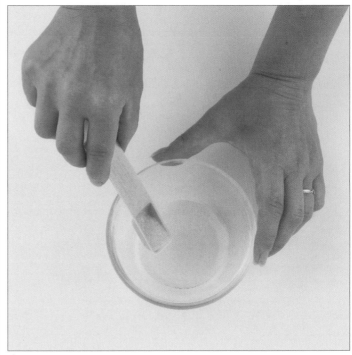

1 Sprinkle 2.5ml/½ tsp gelatine over 15ml/1 tbsp cold water in a small bowl and leave to
"sponge" for 5 minutes. Place the bowl over a pan of hot water and stir until
dissolved. Leave to cool.

Using Cream Alternatives
Serve strained yogurt with puddings
instead of cream, sweetened with a
little honey. Curd (farmers') cheese
can be used instead of cream.

2 Whisk 50ml/2fl oz/¼ cup skimmed
milk powder, 15ml/1 tbsp caster sugar,
15ml/1 tbsp lemon juice and 60ml/4 tbsp
cold water until frothy. Add the dissolved
gelatine and whisk for a few seconds or
more. Chill in the fridge for 30 minutes.

3 Whisk the chilled mixture again until
very thick and frothy. Serve within
30 minutes of making.

Alternatives to Cream

Yogurt is an excellent alternative to whipped cream for decorating cakes and desserts.
Strained yogurt and curd cheese are simple to make at home, and tend to be lower in fat
than commercial varieties.

MAKING YOGURT PIPING CREAM

1 Sprinkle 10ml/2 tsp gelatine over 45ml/3 tbsp cold water in a small bowl and leave to "sponge" for 5 minutes. Place the bowl over a saucepan of hot water and stir until dissolved. Leave to cool.

2 Mix together 300ml/½ pint/1¼ cups yogurt, 15ml/1 tbsp fructose and 2.5ml/½ tsp vanilla essence. Stir in the gelatine. Chill for 30 minutes.

3 Whisk one egg white until stiff and carefully fold it into the yogurt mixture. Spoon into a piping bag fitted with a piping nozzle and use immediately.

MAKING STRAINED YOGURT AND CURD CHEESE

1 Line a sieve with a double layer of muslin. Put over a bowl and pour in 550ml/18fl oz/2½ cups yogurt.

2 Leave to drain in the refrigerator for 3 hours – it will have separated into thick strained yogurt and watery whey.

3 For curd (farmers') cheese, leave to drain in the refrigerator for 8 hours or overnight. Spoon the curd cheese into a bowl, cover and keep chilled until needed.

Cakes

Low in fat doesn't have to
mean low in taste. These
deliciously light cakes
are bursting with flavours
suited to all seasons and
every occasion.

Lemon Chiffon Cake

Lemon mousse provides a tangy filling for this light lemon sponge.

Serves 8
2 eggs
75g/3oz/6 tbsp caster (superfine) sugar
grated rind of 1 lemon
50g/2oz/½ cup sifted plain
(all-purpose) flour
shredded lemon rind, to decorate

For the filling
2 eggs, separated
75g/3oz/6 tbsp caster (superfine) sugar
grated rind and juice of 1 lemon
30ml/2 tbsp water
15ml/1 tbsp gelatine
120ml/4fl oz/½ cup low-fat
fromage frais or cream cheese

For the icing
15ml/1 tbsp lemon juice
115g/4oz/1 cup icing (confectioners')
sugar, sifted

Cook's Tip
The mousse should be just setting when the egg whites are added. Speed up this process by placing the bowl of mousse in iced water.

NUTRITION NOTES
Per portion
Energy   202Kcals/849kJ
Fat   2.81g
Saturated Fat   0.79g
Cholesterol   96.4mg
Fibre   0.2g

1 Preheat the oven to 180°C/350°F/ Gas 4. Grease and line a 20cm/8in loose-bottomed cake tin (pan). Whisk the eggs, sugar and lemon rind together with a hand-held electric whisk until thick and mousse-like. Gently fold in the flour, then turn the mixture into the prepared tin.

2 Bake for 20–25 minutes until the cake springs back when lightly pressed in the centre. Turn on to a wire rack to cool. Once cold, split the cake in half horizontally and return the lower half to the clean cake tin.

3 Make the filling. Put the egg yolks, sugar, lemon rind and juice in a bowl. Beat with a hand-held electric whisk until thick, pale and creamy.

4 Pour the water into a heatproof bowl and sprinkle the gelatine on top. Leave until spongy, then stir over simmering water until dissolved. Cool, then whisk into the yolk mixture. Fold in the fromage frais. When the mixture begins to set, whisk the egg whites to soft peaks. Fold the egg whites into the mousse mixture.

5 Pour the lemon mousse over the sponge in the cake tin, spreading it to the edges. Set the second layer of sponge on top and chill until set.

6 Slide a metal spatula dipped in hot water between the tin and the cake to loosen it. Transfer to a serving plate. To make icing, add enough lemon juice to the icing sugar to make a mixture thick enough to coat the back of a wooden spoon. Pour over the cake and spread to the edges. Decorate with lemon shreds.

Irish Whiskey Cake

This moist, rich fruit cake is drizzled with whiskey as soon as it comes out of the oven.

Serves 12

115g/4oz/½ cup glacé (candied) cherries
175g/6oz/¾ cup dark muscovado
(molasses) sugar
115g/4oz/⅔ cup sultanas (golden raisins)
115g/4oz/⅔ cup raisins
115g/4oz/⅔ cup currants
300ml/½ pint/1¼ cups cold tea
300g/11oz/2⅔ cups self-raising
(self-rising) flour, sifted
1 egg
45ml/3 tbsp Irish whiskey

NUTRITION NOTES

Per portion	
Energy	265Kcals/1115kJ
Fat	0.88g
Saturated Fat	0.25g
Cholesterol	16mg
Fibre	1.48g

---

1 Mix the cherries, sugar, dried fruit and tea in a large bowl. Leave to soak overnight until all the tea has been absorbed into the fruit. Preheat the oven to 180°C/350°F/ Gas 4.

2 Grease and line a 1kg/2¼lb loaf tin (pan). Add the flour, then the egg to the fruit mixture and beat thoroughly until well mixed.

3 Pour the mixture into the prepared tin and bake for 1½ hours or until a skewer inserted into the centre of the cake comes out clean.

4 Prick the top of the cake with a skewer and drizzle over the whiskey while the cake is still hot. Allow to stand for about 5 minutes, then remove from the tin and cool on a wire rack.

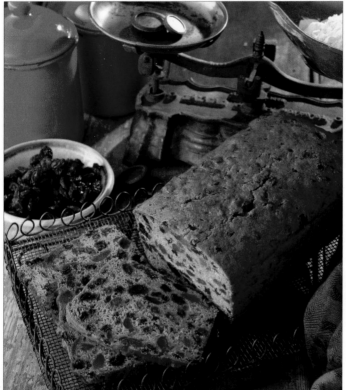

Cook's Tip
If time is short, use hot tea and soak the fruit for just 2 hours.

Angel Cake

A delicious light cake to serve as a dessert for a special occasion.

Serves 10

40g/1½oz/⅓ cup cornflour (cornstarch)
40g/1½oz/⅓ cup plain (all-purpose) flour
8 egg whites
225g/8oz/generous 1 cup caster
(superfine) sugar, plus extra for sprinkling
5ml/1 tsp vanilla essence (extract)
90ml/6 tbsp orange-flavoured glacé
icing, 4–6 physalis and a little icing
(confectioners') sugar, to decorate

1 Preheat the oven to 180°C/350°F/
Gas 4. Sift both flours on to a sheet
of baking parchment.

4 Sprinkle a piece of baking parchment
with caster sugar and set an egg cup
in the centre. Invert the cake tin over the
paper, balancing it carefully on the egg
cup. When cold, the cake will drop out of
the tin. Transfer it to a plate, spoon over
the glacé icing, arrange the physalis
on top and then dust with icing sugar
and serve.

NUTRITION NOTES

Per portion

Energy	139Kcals/582kJ
Fat	0.08g
Saturated Fat	0.1g
Cholesterol	0
Fibre	0.13g

2 Whisk the egg whites in a large
clean, dry bowl until very stiff, then
gradually add the sugar and vanilla
essence, whisking until the mixture is
thick and glossy.

3 Gently fold in the flour mixture with a
large metal spoon. Spoon into an
ungreased 25cm/10in angel cake tin
(pan), smooth the surface and bake for
about 45–50 minutes, until the cake
springs back when lightly pressed.

Tia Maria Gâteau

A feather-light coffee sponge with a creamy liqueur-flavoured filling.

Serves 8

75g/3oz/⅔ cup plain (all-purpose) flour
30ml/2 tbsp instant coffee powder
3 eggs
115g/4oz/generous ½ cup caster
(superfine) sugar
coffee beans, to decorate (optional)

For the filling

175g/6oz/¾ cup low-fat soft cheese
15ml/1 tbsp clear honey
15ml/1 tbsp Tia Maria liqueur
50g/2oz/¼ cup stem ginger,
roughly chopped

For the icing

225g/8oz/2 cups icing (confectioners')
sugar, sifted
10ml/2 tsp coffee essence
15ml/1 tbsp water
5ml/1 tsp reduced-fat cocoa
powder (unsweetened)

Cook's Tip

When folding in the flour mixture
in step 3, be careful not to
remove the air, as it helps the
cake to rise.

NUTRITION NOTES

Per portion
Energy	226Kcals/951kJ
Fat	3.14g
Saturated Fat	1.17g
Cholesterol	75.03mg
Fibre	0.64g

1 Preheat the oven to 190°C/375°F/
Gas 5. Grease and line a 20cm/8in
deep round cake tin (pan). Sift the flour
and coffee powder together on to a sheet
of baking parchment.

2 Whisk the eggs and sugar in a bowl
with a hand-held electric whisk
until thick and mousse-like. (When the
whisk is lifted, a trail should remain on
the surface of the mixture for at least
15 seconds.)

3 Gently fold in the flour mixture with a
metal spoon. Turn the mixture into
the prepared tin. Bake the sponge for
30–35 minutes or until it springs back
when lightly pressed. Turn on to a wire
rack to cool completely.

4 To make the filling, mix the soft
cheese with the honey in a bowl.
Beat until smooth, then stir in the Tia
Maria and chopped stem ginger.

5 Split the cake in half horizontally and
sandwich the two halves together
with the Tia Maria filling.

6 Make the icing. In a bowl, mix the
icing sugar and coffee essence
with enough of the water to make a
consistency that will coat the back of a
wooden spoon. Pour three-quarters of
the icing over the cake, spreading it
evenly to the edges. Stir the cocoa into
the remaining icing until smooth. Spoon
into a piping (pastry) bag fitted with a
writing nozzle and pipe the mocha icing
over the coffee icing. Decorate with
coffee beans, if liked.

Chocolate Banana Cake

A chocolate cake that's deliciously low in fat – it is moist enough to eat without the icing if you want to cut down on calories.

Serves 8
225g/8oz/2 cups self-raising
(self-rising) flour
45ml/3 tbsp reduced-fat cocoa
powder (unsweetened)
115g/4oz/½ cup light muscovado
(brown) sugar
30ml/2 tbsp malt extract
30ml/2 tbsp golden (light corn) syrup
2 eggs
60ml/4 tbsp skimmed milk
60ml/4 tbsp sunflower oil
2 large ripe bananas

For the icing
225g/8oz/2 cups icing (confectioners')
sugar, sifted
35ml/7 tsp reduced-fat cocoa
powder, sifted
15–30ml/1–2 tbsp warm water

1 Preheat the oven to 160°C/325°F/
Gas 3. Grease and line a deep round 20cm/8in cake tin (pan).

2 Sift the flour into a mixing bowl with the cocoa powder. Stir in the sugar.

3 Make a well in the centre and add the malt extract, golden syrup, eggs, milk and oil. Mash the bananas thoroughly and stir them into the mixture until completely combined.

4 Pour the cake mixture into the prepared tin and bake for 1–1¼ hours or until the centre of the cake springs back when lightly pressed.

5 Remove the cake from the tin and leave on a wire rack to cool.

6 Reserve 50g/2oz/½ cup icing sugar and 5ml/1 tsp cocoa powder. Make a dark icing by beating the remaining sugar and cocoa powder with enough of the warm water to make a thick icing. Pour it over the top of the cake and spread evenly to the edges. Make a thinner, lighter icing by mixing the remaining icing sugar and cocoa powder with a few drops of water. Drizzle or pipe this icing across the top of the cake to decorate.

NUTRITION NOTES
Per portion

Energy	411Kcals/1727kJ
Fat	8.791g
Saturated Fat	2.06g
Cholesterol	48.27mg
Fibre	2.06g

Coffee Sponge Drops

These are delicious on their own, but taste even better with a filling made by mixing low-fat soft cheese with drained and chopped stem ginger.

Makes 12
50g/2oz/½ cup plain (all-purpose) flour
15ml/1 tbsp instant coffee powder
2 eggs
75g/3oz/6 tbsp caster (superfine) sugar

For the filling
115g/4oz/½ cup low-fat soft cheese
40g/1½oz/¼ cup chopped preserved
stem ginger

1 Preheat the oven to 190°C/375°F/ Gas 5. Line two baking sheets with baking parchment. Make the filling by beating together the soft cheese and stem ginger. Chill until required. Sift the flour and instant coffee powder together.

3 Carefully add the sifted flour and coffee mixture and gently fold in with a metal spoon, being careful not to knock out any air.

2 Combine the eggs and caster sugar in a bowl. Beat with a hand-held electric whisk until thick and mousse-like. (When the whisk is lifted, a trail should remain on the surface of the mixture for at least 15 seconds.)

4 Spoon the mixture into a piping (pastry) bag fitted with a 1cm/½in plain nozzle. Pipe 4cm/1½in rounds on the baking sheets. Bake for 12 minutes. Cool on a wire rack, then sandwich together with the filling.

Cook's Tip
As an alternative to stem ginger in the filling, try walnuts.

NUTRITION NOTES
Per portion
Energy   69Kcals/290kJ
Fat   1.36g
Saturated Fat   0.5g
Cholesterol   33.33mg
Fibre   0.29g

Chocolate and Orange Angel Cake

This light-as-air sponge with its fluffy icing is virtually fat free, yet tastes heavenly.

Serves 10

25g/1oz/¼ cup plain (all-purpose) flour
15g/½oz/2 tbsp reduced-fat cocoa powder (unsweetened)
15g/½oz/2 tbsp cornflour (cornstarch)
pinch of salt
5 egg whites
2.5ml/½ tsp cream of tartar
115g/4oz/scant ½ cup caster (superfine) sugar
blanched and shredded rind of 1 orange, to decorate

For the icing

200g/7oz/scant 1 cup caster (superfine) sugar
1 egg white

1 Preheat the oven to 180°C/350°F/ Gas 4. Sift the flour, cocoa powder, cornflour and salt together three times. Beat the egg whites in a large clean, dry bowl until foamy. Add the cream of tartar, then whisk until soft peaks form.

2 Add the caster sugar to the egg whites a spoonful at a time, whisking after each addition. Sift a third of the flour and cocoa mixture over the meringue and gently fold in. Repeat, sifting and folding in the flour and cocoa mixture two more times.

3 Spoon the mixture into a non-stick 20cm/8in ring mould and level the top. Bake for 35 minutes or until springy to the touch. Turn upside down on to a wire rack and leave to cool in the tin (pan). Carefully ease out of the tin.

4 For the icing, put the sugar in a pan with 75ml/5 tbsp cold water. Stir over a low heat until dissolved. Boil until the syrup reaches a temperature of 119°C/ 238°F on a sugar thermometer or when a drop of the syrup makes a soft ball when dripped into a cup of cold water. Remove from the heat.

5 Whisk the egg white until stiff. Add the syrup in a thin stream, whisking all the time. Continue to whisk until the mixture is very thick and fluffy.

6 Spread the icing over the top and sides of the cooled cake. Sprinkle the orange rind over the top of the cake and serve.

NUTRITION NOTES

Per portion

Energy	153Kcals/644kJ
Fat	0.27g
Saturated Fat	0.13g
Cholesterol	0
Fibre	0.25g

Apricot and Orange Roulade

This elegant dessert is good served with a spoonful of natural yogurt or crème fraîche.

Serves 6

4 egg whites
115g/4oz/generous ½ cup golden caster
(superfine) sugar
50g/2oz/½ cup plain (all-purpose) flour
finely grated rind of 1 small orange
45ml/3 tbsp orange juice
10ml/2 tsp icing (confectioners') sugar and
shredded orange rind, to decorate

For the filling

115g/4oz/½ cup ready-to-eat dried apricots
150ml/¼ pint/⅔ cup orange juice

NUTRITION NOTES

Per portion	
Energy	203Kcals/853kJ
Fat	10.52g
Saturated Fat	2.05g
Cholesterol	0
Fibre	2.53g

1 Preheat the oven to 200°C/400°F/ Gas 6. Grease a 23 x 33cm/9 x 13in Swiss roll tin (jelly roll pan) and line it with baking parchment. Grease the paper.

2 For the roulade, place the egg whites in a large bowl and whisk them until they hold peaks. Gradually add the sugar, whisking hard between each addition.

3 Fold in the flour, orange rind and juice. Spoon the mixture into the prepared tin and spread it evenly.

4 Bake for about 15–18 minutes, or until the sponge is firm and light golden in colour. Turn out on to a sheet of baking parchment and roll it up Swiss (jelly) roll-style loosely from one short side. Leave to cool.

5 For the filling, roughly chop the apricots, and place them in a pan with the orange juice. Cover the pan and leave to simmer until most of the liquid has been absorbed. Purée the apricots in a food processor or blender.

6 Unroll the roulade and spread with the apricot mixture. Roll up, arrange strips of paper diagonally across the roll, sprinkle lightly with lines of icing sugar, remove the paper and scatter with shredded orange rind to serve.

Cook's Tip

Make and bake the sponge mixture a day in advance and keep it, rolled with the paper, in a cool place. Fill it with the fruit purée 2–3 hours before serving. The sponge can also be frozen for up to 2 months; thaw it at room temperature and fill it as above.

Nectarine Amaretto Cake

Amaretto liqueur adds a hint of luxury to this fruity cake.

1 Preheat the oven to 180°C/350°F/ Gas 4. Grease a 20cm/8in round, loose-bottomed cake tin (pan). Whisk together the egg yolks, caster sugar, lemon rind and juice in a bowl until the mixture is thick, pale and creamy.

2 Fold in the semolina, almonds and flour until smooth.

3 Whisk the egg whites in a bowl until fairly stiff. Use a metal spoon to stir a generous spoonful of the whites into the semolina mixture, then fold in the remaining egg whites. Spoon the mixture into the cake tin.

4 Bake for 30–35 minutes until the centre of the cake springs back when pressed lightly. Remove from the oven and loosen around the edge with a metal spatula. Prick the top with a skewer. Leave to cool in the tin.

5 To make the syrup, heat the sugar and water in a small pan, stirring until the sugar is dissolved. Boil without stirring for 2 minutes. Add the amaretto liqueur and drizzle the liqueur syrup over the cake in the tin.

6 Remove the cake from the tin and transfer to a serving plate. Slice the nectarines and arrange them on top of the cake. Brush with warm apricot glaze.

Serves 8

3 eggs, separated
175g/6oz/¾ cup caster (superfine) sugar
grated rind and juice of 1 lemon
50g/2oz/⅓ cup semolina
25g/1oz/¼ cup ground almonds
25g/1oz/¼ cup plain (all-purpose) flour
2 nectarines, halved and stoned (pitted)
60ml/4 tbsp apricot glaze

For the syrup
45g/3oz/⅓ cup caster (superfine) sugar
90ml/6 tbsp water
30ml/2 tbsp amaretto liqueur

NUTRITION NOTES
Per portion

Energy	264Kcals/1108kJ
Fat	5.7g
Saturated Fat	0.85g
Cholesterol	72.19mg
Fibre	1.08g

Banana and Gingerbread Slices

Very quick to make and deliciously moist due to the addition of bananas.

Serves 20
275g/10oz/2½ cups plain
(all-purpose) flour
20ml/4 tsp ground ginger
10ml/2 tsp mixed (apple pie) spice
5ml/1 tsp bicarbonate of soda
(baking soda)
115g/4oz/½ cup soft light brown sugar
60ml/4 tbsp sunflower oil
30ml/2 tbsp molasses or black treacle
30ml/2 tbsp malt extract
2 eggs
60ml/4 tbsp orange juice
3 ripe bananas
115g/4oz/scant 1 cup raisins

Variation
To make Spiced Honey and
Banana Cake; omit the ground
ginger and add another 5ml/1 tsp
mixed spice; omit the malt extract
and the molasses or treacle and
add 60ml/4 tbsp strong-flavoured
clear honey instead; and replace
the raisins with either sultanas
(golden raisins), coarsely chopped
ready-to-eat dried apricots or
semi-dried pineapple. If you
choose to use the pineapple, then
you could also replace the orange
juice with fresh pineapple juice.

Cook's Tip
The flavour of this cake develops
as it keeps, so if you can, store it
for a few days before eating.

NUTRITION NOTES
Per portion

Energy	148Kcals/621kJ
Fat	3.07g
Saturated Fat	0.53g
Cholesterol	19.3mg
Fibre	0.79g

1 Preheat the oven to 180°C/350°F/
Gas 4. Lightly grease and line an
18 x 28cm/7 x 11in baking tin (pan).

2 Sift the flour into a bowl with the
spices and bicarbonate of soda. Mix
in the sugar with some of the flour and
sift it all into the bowl.

3 Make a well in the centre, add the oil,
molasses or black treacle, malt
extract, eggs and orange juice and mix
together thoroughly.

4 Mash the bananas, then add them
to the bowl with the raisins and mix
together well.

5 Pour the mixture into the prepared
baking tin and bake for about 35–
40 minutes, or until the centre springs
back when lightly pressed.

6 Leave the cake in the tin to cool for
5 minutes, then turn out on to a wire
rack and leave to cool completely. Cut
into 20 slices.

Banana Ginger Parkin

Parkin keeps well and really improves over time. Store it in a covered container for up to two months.

Serves 12

200g/7oz/1¾ cups plain (all-purpose) flour
10ml/2 tsp bicarbonate of soda (baking soda)
10ml/2 tsp ground ginger
150g/5oz/1¼ cups medium oatmeal
60ml/4 tbsp dark muscovado (molasses) sugar
75g/3oz/6 tbsp sunflower margarine
150g/5oz/⅓ cup golden (light corn) syrup
1 egg, beaten
3 ripe bananas, mashed
75g/3oz/¾ cup icing (confectioners') sugar
preserved stem ginger, to decorate

NUTRITION NOTES

Per portion

Energy	277Kcals/1163kJ
Fat	6.9g
Saturated Fat	1.4g
Cholesterol	16.4mg
Fibre	1.72g

1 Preheat the oven to 160°C/325°F/ Gas 3. Grease and line an 18 x 28cm/ 7 x 11in cake tin (pan).

2 Sift together the flour, bicarbonate of soda and ginger, then stir in the oatmeal. Melt the sugar, margarine and syrup in a pan, then stir into the flour mixture. Beat in the egg and mashed bananas.

3 Spoon into the tin and bake for about 1 hour, or until firm to the touch. Allow to cool in the tin, then turn out and cut into squares.

4 Sift the icing sugar into a bowl and stir in just enough water to make a smooth, runny icing. Using a piping (pastry) bag, drizzle the icing over each square and top with a piece of stem ginger, to decorate.

Cook's Tip

This is a nutritious, energy-giving cake that is a really good choice for packed lunches as it doesn't break up too easily.

Spiced Date and Walnut Cake

A classic flavour combination, which makes a very easy low-fat, high-fibre cake.

1 Preheat the oven to 180°C/350°F/
Gas 4. Grease and line a 900g/2lb loaf
tin (pan) with baking parchment.

2 Sift together the flour and spice,
adding back any bran from the sieve.
Stir in the dates and walnuts.

3 Mix the oil, sugar and milk, then stir
evenly into the dry ingredients.

4 Spoon into the prepared tin and
arrange the walnut halves on top.
Bake the cake in the oven for about
45–50 minutes, or until golden brown and
firm. Turn out the cake, remove the lining
paper and leave to cool on a wire rack.

Serves 10

300g/11oz/2⅔ cups wholemeal (whole-
wheat) self-raising (self-rising) flour
10ml/2 tsp mixed (apple pie) spice
150g/5oz/¾ cup chopped dates
50g/2oz/½ cup chopped walnuts
60ml/4 tbsp sunflower oil
115g/4oz/½ cup dark muscovado
(molasses) sugar
300ml/½ pint/1¼ cups skimmed milk
walnut halves, to decorate

NUTRITION NOTES

Per portion

Energy	265Kcals/1114kJ
Fat	9.27g
Saturated Fat	1.14g
Cholesterol	0.6mg
Fibre	3.51g

Cook's Tip

Pecan nuts can be used in place of
the walnuts in this cake.

Greek Honey and Lemon Cake

Moist and tangy, a delicious tea-time treat.

Makes 16 slices

40g/1½oz/3 tbsp sunflower margarine
60ml/4 tbsp clear honey
finely grated rind and juice of 1 lemon
150ml/¼ pint/⅔ cup skimmed milk
150g/5oz/1¼ cups plain (all-purpose) flour
7.5ml/1½ tsp baking powder
2.5ml/½ tsp grated nutmeg
50g/2oz/⅓ cup semolina
2 egg whites
10ml/2 tsp sesame seeds

NUTRITION NOTES

Per portion

Energy	82Kcals/342kJ
Fat	2.62g
Saturated Fat	0.46g
Cholesterol	0.36mg
Fibre	0.41g

1 Preheat the oven to 200°C/400°F/ Gas 6. Lightly oil a 19cm/7½in square deep cake tin (pan) and line the base with parchment paper.

2 Place the margarine and 45ml/3 tbsp of the honey in a pan and heat gently until melted. Reserve 15ml/1 tbsp lemon juice, then stir in the rest with the rind and milk. Transfer to a mixing bowl.

3 Add the flour, baking powder and nutmeg and stir through. Gradually beat the semolina into the mixture. Whisk the egg whites until they form soft peaks, then fold evenly into the mixture.

4 Spoon into the tin and sprinkle with sesame seeds. Bake the cake for 25–30 minutes, until golden brown. Mix together the reserved honey and lemon juice and drizzle over the cake while warm. Cool in the tin, then cut into 16 fingers to serve.

Strawberry Roulade

A creamy fruit filling is delicious in a light roulade.

1 Preheat the oven to 200°C/400°F/ Gas 6. Oil a 23 x 33cm/9 x 13in Swiss roll tin (jelly roll pan) and line with baking parchment.

2 Place the egg whites in a large bowl and whisk until they form soft peaks. Gradually whisk in the sugar. Fold in half of the sifted flour, then fold in the rest with the orange juice.

3 Spoon the mixture into the prepared tin, spreading evenly. Bake for 15– 18 minutes, or until golden brown and firm to the touch.

4 Meanwhile, spread out a sheet of baking parchment and sprinkle with caster sugar. Turn out the cake on to this and remove the lining paper. Roll up the sponge loosely from one short side, with the paper inside. Cool.

5 Unroll and remove the paper. Stir the strawberries into the fromage frais and spread over the sponge. Re-roll and serve decorated with strawberries.

Serves 6
4 egg whites
115g/4oz/generous ½ cup golden caster (superfine) sugar, plus extra for sprinkling
75g/3oz/⅔ cup plain (all-purpose) flour, sifted
30ml/2 tbsp orange juice
115g/4oz/1 cup strawberries, chopped
150g/5oz/⅔ cup low-fat fromage frais or low-fat cream cheese
strawberries, to decorate

NUTRITION NOTES
Per portion

Energy	154Kcals/646kJ
Fat	0.24g
Saturated Fat	0.01g
Cholesterol	0.25mg
Fibre	0.61g

Peach Roll

A feather-light sponge enclosing peach jam – delicious at tea time.

Serves 6–8
3 eggs
115g/4oz/generous ½ cup caster
(superfine) sugar, plus extra
for sprinkling
75g/3oz/⅔ cup plain (all-purpose)
flour, sifted
15ml/1 tbsp boiling water
90ml/6 tbsp peach jam
glacé icing (see Cook's Tip) or
icing (confectioners') sugar,
for dusting (optional)

Cook's Tip

To decorate the Swiss roll with
glacé icing, make the icing with
115g/4oz/1 cup icing sugar and
enough warm water to make a thin
glacé icing. Put in a piping (pastry)
bag fitted with a small writing
nozzle and pipe lines over the top.

NUTRITION NOTES

Per portion	
Energy	178Kcals/746kJ
Fat	2.54g
Saturated Fat	0.67g
Cholesterol	82.5mg
Fibre	0.33g

1 Preheat the oven to 200°C/400°F/
Gas 6. Grease a 30 x 20cm/12 x 8in
Swiss roll tin (jelly roll pan) and line with
baking parchment. Combine the eggs and
sugar in a bowl. Beat with a hand-held
electric whisk until thick and mousse-like.
(When the whisk is lifted, a trail should
remain on the surface of the mixture for
at least 15 seconds.)

2 Carefully fold in the flour with a large
metal spoon, then add the boiling
water in the same way.

3 Spoon into the prepared tin, spread
evenly to the edges and bake for
about 10–12 minutes until the cake
springs back when lightly pressed.

4 Spread a sheet of baking parchment
on a flat surface, sprinkle it with
caster sugar, then invert the cake on top.
Peel off the lining paper.

5 Neatly trim the edges of the cake.
Make a neat cut two-thirds of the
way through the cake, about 1cm/½in
from the short edge nearest you.

6 Spread the cake with the peach jam
and roll up quickly from the partially
cut end. Hold in position for a minute,
making sure the join is underneath. Cool
on a wire rack. Decorate with glacé icing
or dust with icing sugar before serving.

Spiced Apple Cake

Grated apple and chopped dates give this cake a natural sweetness.

Serves 8

225g/8oz/2 cups self-raising (self-rising) wholemeal (whole-wheat) flour
5ml/1 tsp baking powder
10ml/2 tsp ground cinnamon
175g/6oz/1 cup chopped dates
2 eating apples
75g/3oz/scant ½ cup light muscovado (brown) sugar
15ml/1 tbsp pear and apple spread
120ml/4fl oz/½ cup apple juice
2 eggs
90ml/6 tbsp sunflower oil
15ml/1 tbsp chopped walnuts

NUTRITION NOTES

Per portion

Energy	331Kcals/1389kJ
Fat	11.41g
Saturated Fat	1.68g
Cholesterol	48.13mg
Fibre	2.5g

1 Preheat the oven to 180°C/350°F/ Gas 4. Grease and line a deep round 20cm/8in cake tin (pan). Sift the flour, baking powder and cinnamon into a mixing bowl, then mix in the dates and make a well in the centre. Core and grate the apples.

2 Mix the sugar with the pear and apple spread in a small bowl. Gradually stir in the apple juice. Add to the dry ingredients with the eggs, oil and grated apples. Mix thoroughly.

3 Spoon the mixture into the prepared cake tin, sprinkle liberally with the walnuts and bake for 60–65 minutes or until a skewer inserted into the centre of the cake comes out clean. Transfer to a wire rack, remove the lining paper and leave to cool.

Cook's Tip

Omit 25g/1oz/2 tbsp sugar if the fruit is very sweet. It is not necessary to peel the apples – the skin adds extra fibre and softens on cooking.

Fruit and Nut Cake

This rich fruit cake is best left for two to three weeks before cutting.

1 Preheat the oven to 160°C/325°F/
Gas 3. Grease and line a deep round
20cm/8in cake tin (pan). Secure a band
of brown paper around the outside.

2 Sift the flours into a mixing bowl
together with the mixed spice and
make a well in the centre.

3 Put the apple and apricot spread in a
small bowl. Gradually stir in the
honey and molasses or treacle. Add to
the dry ingredients with the oil, orange
juice, eggs and mixed fruit. Mix thoroughly.

4 Turn the mixture into the prepared tin
and smooth the surface. Arrange the
almonds and cherries in a pattern over the
top. Bake for 2 hours or until a skewer
inserted into the centre comes out clean.

5 Transfer to a wire rack until cold, then
lift out of the tin and remove the
paper. Store for up to 3 months wrapped
in greaseproof paper, then in foil, in a
cool, dry place.

Serves 12–14
175g/6oz/1½ cups self-raising (self-
rising) wholemeal (whole-wheat) flour
175g/6oz/1½ cups self-raising
(self-rising) white flour
10ml/2 tsp mixed (apple pie) spice
15ml/1 tbsp apple and apricot or other
fruit spread
45ml/3 tbsp clear honey
15ml/1 tbsp molasses or black treacle
90ml/6 tbsp sunflower oil
175ml/6fl oz/¾ cup orange juice
2 eggs, beaten
675g/1½lb/4 cups luxury mixed dried fruit
45ml/3 tbsp split almonds
50g/2oz/¼ cup glacé (candied)
cherries, halved

NUTRITION NOTES

Per portion
Energy	333Kcals/1400kJ
Fat	8.54g
Saturated Fat	1.12g
Cholesterol	29.62mg
Fibre	3.08g

Eggless Christmas Cake

A deliciously clever way to create a low-calorie Christmas treat.

Serves 12

75g/3oz/⅓ cup glacé (candied) cherries
75g/3oz/½ cup sultanas (golden raisins)
75g/3oz/generous ½ cup raisins
75g/3oz/⅓ cup currants
50g/2oz/⅓ cup cut mixed peel
250ml/8fl oz/1 cup apple juice
25g/1oz/2 tbsp toasted hazelnuts
30ml/2 tbsp pumpkin seeds
2 pieces preserved stem ginger in
syrup, chopped
finely grated rind of 1 lemon
120ml/4fl oz/½ cup skimmed milk
120ml/4fl oz/½ cup sunflower oil
225g/8oz/2 cups wholemeal (whole-
wheat) self-raising (self-rising) flour
10ml/2 tsp mixed (apple pie) spice
45ml/3 tbsp brandy or dark rum
apricot jam, for brushing
glacé (candied) fruits, to decorate

1 Halve the cherries and place them with the sultanas, raisins, currants and mixed peel in a bowl. Stir in the apple juice, cover and leave to soak overnight.

2 Preheat the oven to 150°C/300°F/ Gas 2.

3 Lightly grease and line an 18cm/7in square cake tin (pan).

4 Add the hazelnuts, pumpkin seeds, ginger and lemon rind to the soaked fruit. Stir in the milk and oil. Sift the flour and spice. Stir in with the brandy or rum.

5 Spoon into the prepared tin and bake for 1½ hours, or until golden brown and firm to the touch. Turn out and cool on a wire rack. Brush with sieved apricot jam and decorate with glacé fruits.

NUTRITION NOTES

Per portion

Energy	225Kcals/946kJ
Fat	6.13g
Saturated Fat	0.89g
Cholesterol	0.2mg
Fibre	2.45g

Cranberry and Apple Ring

Tangy cranberries add an unusual flavour to this low-fat cake. It is best eaten very fresh.

Serves 8
225g/8oz/2 cups self-raising
(self-rising) flour
5ml/1 tsp ground cinnamon
75g/3oz/scant ½ cup light muscovado
(brown) sugar
1 crisp eating apple, cored and diced
75g/3oz/½ cup fresh or frozen cranberries
60ml/4 tbsp sunflower oil
150ml/¼ pint/⅔ cup apple juice
apple slices dipped in lemon, and
cranberry jelly, to decorate

1 Preheat the oven to 180°C/350°F/
Gas 4. Lightly grease a 1 litre/1¾ pint/
4 cup ring mould with oil.

2 Sift together the flour and ground
cinnamon, then stir in the sugar.

4 Spoon the mixture into the prepared
ring mould and bake for about 35–
40 minutes, or until the cake is firm to
the touch. Turn out and leave to cool
completely on a wire rack.

5 To serve, decorate the cake with
apple slices, then drizzle with
warmed cranberry jelly.

NUTRITION NOTES
Per portion

Energy	202Kcals/848kJ
Fat	5.91g
Saturated Fat	0.76g
Cholesterol	0
Fibre	1.55g

3 Toss together the diced apple and
cranberries. Stir into the dry
ingredients, then add the oil and apple
juice and beat well.

Cook's Tip
Fresh cranberries are available
throughout the winter months and if
you don't use them all at once, they
can be frozen for up to a year.

Carrot Cake with Lemon Frosting

Lemon frosting is the perfect topping for this all-time favourite.

Serves 8

225g/8oz/2 cups self-raising (self-rising)
wholemeal (whole-wheat) flour
10ml/2 tsp ground allspice
115g/4oz/½ cup light muscovado
(brown) sugar
2 medium carrots, grated
50g/2oz/⅓ cup sultanas (golden raisins)
75ml/5 tbsp sunflower oil
75ml/5 tbsp orange juice
75ml/5 tbsp skimmed milk
2 egg whites

For the frosting

175g/6oz/¾ cup skimmed
milk soft cheese
finely grated rind of ½ lemon
30ml/2 tbsp clear honey
shredded lemon rind, to decorate

NUTRITION NOTES

Per portion

Energy	272Kcals/1146kJ
Fat	7.72g
Saturated Fat	1.04g
Cholesterol	0.4mg
Fibre	3.33g

1 Preheat the oven to 180°C/350°F/
Gas 4. Grease a deep 18cm/7in round
cake tin (pan) and line the base with
baking parchment.

2 Sift the flour and spice together,
then stir in the sugar, grated carrots
and sultanas.

3 Mix the liquids, then stir into the dry
ingredients. Whisk the egg whites
until stiff, then fold in evenly. Spoon into
the tin and bake for 45–50 minutes.

4 Turn out and cool. For the frosting,
beat together the cheese, lemon rind
and honey until smooth. Spread over the
top of the cooled cake, swirling with a
metal spatula. Decorate with lemon rind.

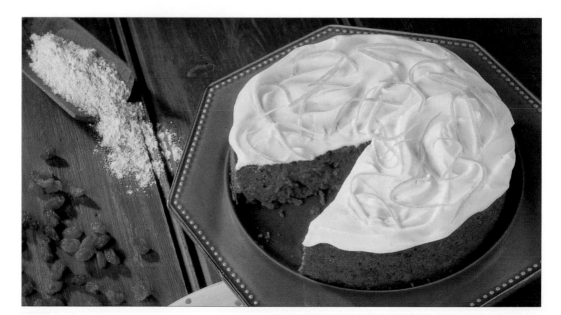

Chewy Fruit Muesli Slice

Low in fat and high in fibre . . . and delicious as well.

Makes 8 slices
75g/3oz/scant ½ cup ready-to-eat dried apricots, chopped
1 eating apple, cored and grated
150g/5oz/1¼ cups Swiss-style muesli
150ml/¼ pint/⅔ cup apple juice
15g/½oz/1 tbsp soft sunflower margarine

1 Preheat the oven to 190°C/375°F/ Gas 5. Place all the ingredients in a large bowl and mix well. Press the mixture into a 20cm/8in round, non-stick sandwich tin (pan) and bake for 35–40 minutes, or until lightly browned and firm.

2 Mark the muesli slice into eight wedges and leave to cool in the tin.

NUTRITION NOTES
Per portion

Energy	112Kcals/467kJ
Fat	2.75g
Saturated Fat	0.48g
Cholesterol	0.13mg
Fibre	2.09g

Ginger Cake with Spiced Cream

A spicy and comforting cake, ideal for winter evenings.

Serves 9

175g/6oz/1½ cups plain (all-purpose) flour
10ml/2 tsp baking powder
2.5ml/½ tsp salt
10ml/2 tsp ground ginger
10ml/2 tsp ground cinnamon
5ml/1 tsp ground cloves
1.5ml/¼ tsp freshly ground nutmeg
2 eggs
200g/7oz/1 cup granulated sugar
250ml/8fl oz/1 cup whipping cream
5ml/1 tsp vanilla essence (extract)
icing (confectioners') sugar, to decorate

For the spiced whipped cream

175ml/6fl oz/¾ cup low-fat
whipping cream
5ml/1 tsp icing (confectioners') sugar
1.5ml/¼ tsp ground cinnamon
1.5ml/¼ tsp ground ginger
0.75ml/⅛ tsp freshly grated nutmeg

1 Preheat the oven to 180°C/350°F/ Gas 4. Grease a 23cm/9in square baking tin (pan).

2 Sift the flour, baking powder, salt, ginger, cinnamon, cloves and nutmeg into a bowl. Set aside.

3 With an electric mixer, beat the eggs on a high speed until very thick, for about 5 minutes. Gradually beat in the granulated sugar.

4 With the mixer on a low speed, beat in the flour mixture alternately with the cream into the eggs, beginning and ending with the flour. Stir in the vanilla.

5 Pour into the tin and bake for 35–40 minutes, until the top springs back when touched lightly. Leave to cool in the tin on a wire rack for 10 minutes.

6 To make the spiced whipped cream, combine the ingredients in a bowl and whip until the cream holds soft peaks. Sprinkle icing sugar over the hot cake, cut into nine squares and serve with the spiced whipped cream.

NUTRITION NOTES

Per portion

Energy	305Kcals/1282kJ
Fat	11.6g
Saturated Fat	6.6g
Cholesterol	69mg
Fibre	0.8g

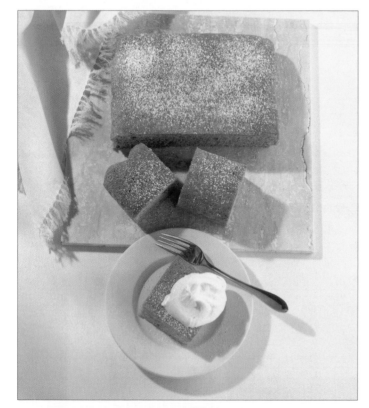

Apple and Pear Skillet Cake

An unusual but delicious cake, prepared on the hob and then baked in the oven.

1 Preheat the oven to 190°C/375°F/ Gas 5. In a mixing bowl, toss together the apple slices, pear slices, walnuts, cinnamon and nutmeg. Set aside.

2 With an electric mixer, beat together the eggs, flour, brown sugar, milk and vanilla.

3 Melt the butter or margarine in a 23cm or 25cm/9in or 10in ovenproof skillet (preferably cast iron) over a medium heat. Add the apple mixture. Cook until lightly caramelized, for about 5 minutes, stirring occasionally.

4 Pour the batter over the fruit and nuts. Transfer the skillet to the oven and bake for about 30 minutes, until the cake is puffy and pulling away from the sides of the pan.

5 Sprinkle the cake lightly with icing sugar and serve hot.

Serves 6

1 apple, peeled, cored and thinly sliced
1 pear, peeled, cored and thinly sliced
50g/2oz/½ cup walnut pieces, chopped
5ml/1 tsp ground cinnamon
5ml/1 tsp freshly grated nutmeg
3 eggs
75g/3oz/⅔ cup plain (all-purpose) flour
30ml/2 tbsp light brown sugar
175ml/6fl oz/¾ cup skimmed milk
5ml/1 tsp vanilla essence (extract)
60ml/4 tbsp butter or margarine
icing (confectioners') sugar, for sprinkling

NUTRITION NOTES

Per portion

Energy	315Kcals/1311kJ
Fat	19.9g
Saturated Fat	3.3g
Cholesterol	98mg
Fibre	1.8g

Cinnamon Apple Gâteau

Make this lovely cake for an autumn celebration.

Serves 6
3 eggs
115g/4oz/generous ½ cup caster
(superfine) sugar
75g/3oz/⅔ cup plain (all-purpose) flour
5ml/1 tsp ground cinnamon

For the filling and topping
4 large eating apples
60ml/4 tbsp clear honey
15ml/1 tbsp water
75g/3oz/½ cup sultanas (golden raisins)
2.5ml/½ tsp ground cinnamon
350g/12oz/1½ cups low-fat soft cheese
45ml/3 tbsp reduced-fat fromage frais
or natural (plain) yogurt
10ml/2 tsp lemon juice
45ml/3 tbsp apricot glaze (see Cook's Tip)
mint sprigs, to decorate

Cook's Tip
Apricot glaze is useful for brushing over a fresh fruit topping or filling. Place a few spoonfuls of apricot jam in a small pan along with a squeeze of lemon juice. Heat the jam, stirring until it is melted and runny. Pour the melted jam into a wire sieve set over a bowl. Stir the jam with a wooden spoon to help it go through. Return the strained jam to the pan. Keep the glaze warm until needed.

NUTRITION NOTES

Per portion	
Energy	203Kcals/853kJ
Fat	10.52g
Saturated Fat	2.05g
Cholesterol	0
Fibre	2.53g

1 Preheat the oven to 190°C/375°F/ Gas 5. Grease and line a 23cm/9in sandwich cake tin (pan). Place the eggs and caster sugar in a bowl and beat with a hand-held electric whisk until thick and mousse-like. (When the whisk is lifted, a trail should remain on the surface of the mixture for at least 15 seconds.)

2 Sift the flour and cinnamon over the egg mixture and fold in with a large metal spoon. Pour into the prepared tin and bake for 25–30 minutes or until the cake springs back when lightly pressed. Turn the cake on to a wire rack to cool.

3 To make the filling, peel, core and slice three of the apples and put them in a pan. Add 30ml/2 tbsp of the honey and the water. Cover and cook over a gentle heat for about 10 minutes. Add the sultanas and cinnamon, stir well, replace the lid and leave to cool.

4 Put the soft cheese in a bowl with the remaining honey, the fromage frais and half the lemon juice. Beat until the mixture is smooth.

5 Halve the cake horizontally, place the bottom half on a board and drizzle over any liquid from the apples. Spread with two-thirds of the cheese mixture, then top with the apple filling. Fit the top of the cake in place.

6 Swirl the remaining cheese mixture over the top of the sponge. Core and slice the remaining apple, sprinkle with lemon juice and use to decorate the edge of the cake. Brush the apple with the apricot glaze and place mint sprigs on top, to decorate.

Scones,
Muffins,
Buns and
Cookies

Served warm and straight
from the oven, these bite-
size bakes are a pleasure
for the palate – with the
added health benefit of
reduced-fat content.

Blueberry Muffins

A real old favourite – and they are not high in calories or fat.

Makes 12

150g/5oz/1¼ cups plain
(all-purpose) flour
50g/2oz/¼ cup granulated sugar
10ml/2 tsp baking powder
2.5ml/½ tsp salt
2 eggs
60ml/4 tbsp butter, melted
175ml/6fl oz/¾ cup skimmed milk
5ml/1 tsp vanilla essence (extract)
5ml/1 tsp grated lemon rind
115g/4oz/1 cup fresh blueberries

NUTRITION NOTES

Per portion

Energy	124Kcals/524kJ
Fat	3.9g
Saturated Fat	0.8g
Cholesterol	33mg
Fibre	0.8g

1 Preheat the oven to 200°C/400°F/ Gas 6.

2 Grease a 12-cup muffin tin (pan) or use paper cases.

3 Sift the flour, sugar, baking powder and salt into a bowl.

4 In another bowl, whisk the eggs until blended. Add the melted butter, milk, vanilla essence and lemon rind and stir to combine. Make a well in the dry ingredients and pour in the egg mixture. With a large metal spoon, stir just until the flour is moistened, not until smooth.

5 Fold in the blueberries.

6 Spoon the batter into the cups, leaving room for the muffins to rise. Bake for 20–25 minutes, or until well risen and firm in the middle. Allow to cool in the tin for about 5 minutes before turning out.

Apple Cranberry Muffins

Fruit and nuts are a winning combination in these mouthwatering muffins.

1 Preheat the oven to 180°C/350°F/ Gas 4. Grease a 12-cup muffin tin (pan) or use paper cases.

2 Melt the butter or margarine over gentle heat. Set aside to cool.

3 Place the egg in a mixing bowl and whisk lightly. Add the melted butter or margarine and whisk to combine.

4 Add the sugar, orange rind and juice. Whisk to blend, then set aside. In a large bowl, sift together the flour, baking powder, bicarbonate of soda, cinnamon, nutmeg, allspice, ginger and salt. Set aside.

5 Quarter, core and peel the apples. Then dice coarsely, using a sharp knife.

6 Make a well in the dry ingredients and pour in the egg mixture. With a spoon, stir until just blended. Add the apples, cranberries and walnuts and stir to blend.

7 Fill the muffin cups three-quarters full and bake for 25–30 minutes, or until well risen and firm in the middle. Transfer the muffins to a rack to cool. Dust lightly with icing sugar before serving, if you wish.

Makes 12

60ml/4 tbsp butter or margarine
1 egg
175g/6oz/scant 1 cup granulated sugar
grated rind of 1 large orange
120ml/4fl oz/½ cup fresh orange juice
175g/6oz/1½ cups plain (all-purpose) flour
2.5ml/½ tsp baking powder
2.5ml/½ tsp bicarbonate of soda
(baking soda)
5ml/1 tsp ground cinnamon
2.5ml/½ tsp freshly grated nutmeg
2.5ml/½ tsp ground allspice
1.5ml/¼ tsp ground ginger
1.5ml/¼ tsp salt
1–2 eating apples
115g/4oz/1 cup cranberries
50g/2oz/½ cup chopped walnuts
icing (confectioners') sugar, for dusting

NUTRITION NOTES

Per portion	
Energy	175Kcals/733kJ
Fat	9.1g
Saturated Fat	1.4g
Cholesterol	16mg
Fibre	1.4g

Raspberry Muffins

These American muffins are made using baking powder and low-fat buttermilk, giving them a light and spongy texture. They are delicious to eat at any time of the day.

Makes 10–12

275g/10oz/2½ cups plain (all-purpose) flour
15ml/1 tbsp baking powder
115g/4oz/generous ½ cup caster (superfine) sugar
1 egg
250ml/8fl oz/1 cup buttermilk
60ml/4 tbsp sunflower oil
150g/5oz/scant 1 cup raspberries

NUTRITION NOTES
Per portion
Energy	171Kcals/719kJ
Fat	4.55g
Saturated Fat	0.71g
Cholesterol	16.5mg
Fibre	1.02g

1 Preheat the oven to 200°C/400°F/ Gas 6. Grease a 12-cup muffin tin (pan) or use paper cases. Sift the flour and baking powder into a mixing bowl, stir in the sugar, then make a well in the centre.

2 Mix the egg, buttermilk and sunflower oil together in a bowl, pour into the flour mixture and mix quickly.

3 Add the raspberries and lightly fold in with a metal spoon. Spoon the mixture into the tin or paper cases.

4 Bake the muffins for 20–25 minutes until golden brown and firm in the middle. Transfer to a wire rack and serve warm or cold.

Spiced Banana Muffins

These light and nutritious muffins include banana for added fibre, and make a tasty tea-time treat.
If liked, slice off the tops and fill with jam.

Makes 12
75g/3oz/⅔ cup plain (all-purpose)
wholemeal (whole-wheat) flour
50g/2oz/½ cup plain (all-purpose)
white flour
10ml/2 tsp baking powder
pinch of salt
5ml/1 tsp mixed (apple pie) spice
40g/1½oz/3 tbsp soft light brown sugar
50g/2oz/¼ cup polyunsaturated
margarine
1 egg, beaten
150ml/¼ pint/⅔ cup semi-skimmed milk
grated rind of 1 orange
1 ripe banana
20g/¾oz/¼ cup porridge oats
20g/¾oz/scant ¼ cup chopped hazelnuts

1 Preheat the oven to 200°C/400°F/Gas 6. Grease a 12-cup muffin tin (pan) or use paper cases. Sift together both flours, the baking powder, salt and mixed spice into a bowl, then tip the bran remaining in the sieve into the bowl. Stir in the sugar.

2 Melt the margarine and pour it into a mixing bowl. Cool slightly, then beat in the egg, milk and grated orange rind.

4 Spoon the mixture into the tin or paper cases. Combine the oats and hazelnuts and sprinkle a little of the mixture over each muffin.

5 Bake in the preheated oven for 20 minutes until the muffins are well risen and golden, and a skewer inserted in the centre comes out clean. Transfer to a wire rack and allow to cool. These muffins can be served warm or cold.

NUTRITION NOTES

Per portion

Energy	139Kcals/582kJ
Fat	5g
Saturated Fat	1g
Cholesterol	0
Fibre	0.13g

3 Gently fold in the dry ingredients. Mash the banana with a fork, then stir it gently into the mixture, being careful not to overmix.

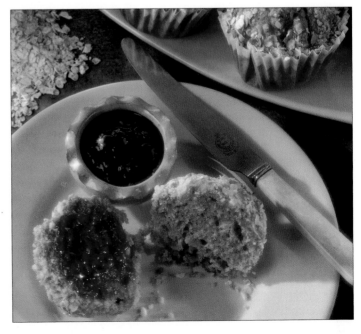

Carrot Muffins

Moist and full of flavour, these unusual muffins are a must.

Makes 12

175g/6oz/¾ cup margarine, at room temperature
75g/3oz/scant ½ cup soft dark brown sugar
1 egg
15ml/1 tbsp water
150g/5oz/2 cups grated carrots
150g/5oz/1¼ cups plain (all-purpose) flour
5ml/1 tsp baking powder
2.5ml/½ tsp bicarbonate of soda (baking soda)
5ml/1 tsp ground cinnamon
1.5ml/¼ tsp freshly grated nutmeg
2.5ml/½ tsp salt

NUTRITION NOTES

Per portion

Energy	155Kcals/647kJ
Fat	9.2g
Saturated Fat	1.8g
Cholesterol	13mg
Fibre	0.8g

1 Preheat the oven to 180°C/350°F/Gas 4. Grease a 12-cup muffin tin (pan) or use paper cases.

2 With an electric mixer, cream the margarine and sugar until they are light and fluffy. Beat in the egg and water. Stir in the carrots.

3 Sift over the flour, baking powder, bicarbonate of soda, cinnamon, nutmeg and salt. Stir to blend.

4 Spoon the batter into the prepared muffin cups, filling them almost to the top. Bake for about 35 minutes, until well risen and firm in the middle. Leave to stand for 10 minutes before transferring to a rack.

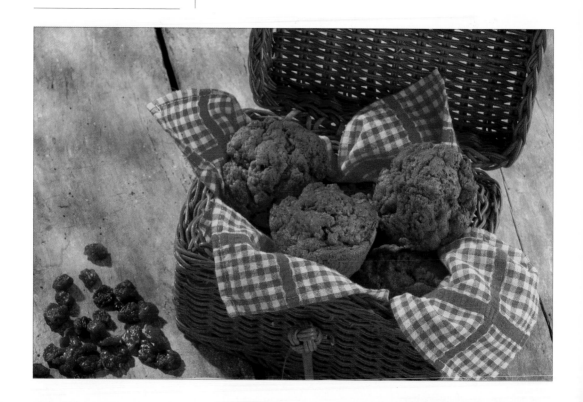

Dried Cherry Muffins

Muffins make a wonderful breakfast, particularly on special occasions.

1 In a mixing bowl, combine the yogurt and cherries. Cover and let stand for 30 minutes. Preheat the oven to 180°C/350°F/Gas 4. Grease a 16-cup muffin tin (pan) or use paper cases.

2 With an electric mixer, cream the butter and sugar together until they are light and fluffy.

3 Add the eggs, one at a time, beating well after each addition.

4 Add the vanilla essence and the cherry mixture and stir to blend. Set aside. In another bowl, sift together the flour, baking powder, bicarbonate of soda and salt. Fold into the cherry mixture in three batches; do not overmix.

5 Fill the prepared muffin cups two-thirds full. For even baking, half-fill any empty cups with water. Bake for about 20 minutes, or until well risen and firm in the middle. Transfer to a rack.

Makes 16

225g/8oz/1 cup natural (plain) yogurt
225g/8oz/1 cup dried cherries
115g/4oz/½ cup butter
175g/6oz/scant 1 cup caster (superfine) sugar
2 eggs
5ml/1 tsp vanilla essence (extract)
200g/7oz/1¾ cups plain (all-purpose) flour
30ml/2 tbsp baking powder
5ml/1 tsp bicarbonate of soda (baking soda)
0.75ml/⅛ tsp salt

NUTRITION NOTES

Per portion	
Energy	197Kcals/826kJ
Fat	6.8g
Saturated Fat	1.4g
Cholesterol	25mg
Fibre	0.7g

Oatmeal Buttermilk Muffins

Add a Scottish flavour to your tea-time table.

Makes 12

75g/3oz/scant 1 cup rolled oats
250ml/8fl oz/1 cup buttermilk
115g/4oz/½ cup butter
75g/3oz/scant ½ cup soft dark
brown sugar
1 egg
115g/4oz/1 cup plain (all-purpose) flour
5ml/1 tsp baking powder
2.5ml/½ tsp salt
25g/1oz/¼ cup raisins

NUTRITION NOTES

Per portion

Energy	213Kcals/893kJ
Fat	9.3g
Saturated Fat	1.9g
Cholesterol	17mg
Fibre	1.2g

1 In a bowl, combine the oats and buttermilk and allow to soak for 1 hour.

2 Grease a 12-cup muffin tin (pan) or use paper cases.

3 Preheat the oven to 200°C/400°F/ Gas 6. With an electric mixer, cream the butter and sugar until light and fluffy. Beat in the egg.

4 In another bowl, sift together the flour, baking powder and salt. Stir the dry ingredients into the butter mixture, alternating with the oat mixture. Fold in the raisins, taking care not to overmix.

5 Fill the prepared cups two-thirds full. Bake for about 20–25 minutes, until a cake tester or skewer inserted in the centre comes out clean. Transfer to a wire rack to cool.

Pumpkin Muffins

Pumpkin has a mild, sweet flavour and makes a delicious, moist muffin.

1 Preheat the oven to 200°C/400°F/ Gas 6. Grease a 14-cup muffin tin (pan) or use paper cases. With an electric mixer, cream the butter or margarine until soft. Add the sugar and molasses and beat until light and fluffy.

2 Add the egg and pumpkin and stir until well blended. Sift over the flour, salt, bicarbonate of soda, cinnamon and nutmeg. Fold just enough to blend; do not overmix.

3 Fold in the currants or raisins. Spoon the batter into the prepared muffin cups, filling them three-quarters full.

4 Bake for about 12–15 minutes, until well risen and firm in the middle. Transfer to a rack. Serve warm or cold.

Makes 14

115g/4oz/½ cup butter or margarine
165g/5½oz/⅔ cup soft dark brown sugar
150ml/¼ pint/⅔ cup molasses
1 egg, beaten
225g/8oz/1 cup cooked or
canned pumpkin
200g/7oz/1⅜ cups plain (all-purpose) flour
1.5ml/¼ tsp salt
5ml/1 tsp bicarbonate of soda
(baking soda)
7.5ml/1½ tsp ground cinnamon
5ml/1 tsp freshly grated nutmeg
25g/1oz/2 tbsp currants or raisins

NUTRITION NOTES
Per portion

Energy	196Kcals/821kJ
Fat	7.3g
Saturated Fat	1.4g
Cholesterol	14mg
Fibre	0.8g

Raisin Bran Muffins

High in fibre and high in flavour, a real treat.

Makes 15
60ml/4 tbsp butter or margarine
75g/3oz/⅔ cup plain (all-purpose) white flour
50g/2oz/½ cup plain (all-purpose) wholemeal (whole-wheat) flour
7.5ml/1½ tsp bicarbonate of soda (baking soda)
0.75ml/⅛ tsp salt
5ml/1 tsp ground cinnamon
40g/1½oz/½ cup bran
75g/3oz/generous ½ cup raisins
50g/2oz/¼ cup soft dark brown sugar
50g/2oz/¼ cup granulated sugar
1 egg
250ml/8fl oz/1 cup buttermilk
juice of ½ lemon

1 Preheat the oven to 200°C/400°F/ Gas 6. Grease a 15-cup muffin tin (pan) or use paper cases.

2 Place the butter or margarine in a heavy pan and melt over a gentle heat.

3 In a mixing bowl, sift together the plain flour, wholemeal flour, bicarbonate of soda, salt and cinnamon.

4 Add the bran, raisins and sugars and stir until blended.

5 In another bowl, mix together the egg, buttermilk, lemon juice and melted butter.

6 Add the buttermilk mixture to the dry ingredients. Stir lightly and quickly until just moistened; do not mix until smooth as this will ruin the texture.

7 Spoon the batter into the prepared muffin cups, filling them almost to the top. Half-fill any empty cups with water before placing in the oven.

8 Bake until golden, for 15–20 minutes. Serve at room temperature.

NUTRITION NOTES

Per portion

Energy	131Kcals/551kJ
Fat	4.1g
Saturated Fat	0.9g
Cholesterol	13mg
Fibre	1.7g

Prune Muffins

All sorts of fruit can be used to make a delicious filling for muffins – prunes are a healthy option.

Makes 12

1 egg
250ml/8fl oz/1 cup skimmed milk
50ml/2fl oz/¼ cup vegetable oil
50g/2oz/¼ cup granulated sugar
30ml/2 tbsp soft dark brown sugar
225g/8oz/2 cups plain
(all-purpose) flour
30ml/2 tsp baking powder
2.5ml/½ tsp salt
1.5ml/¼ tsp freshly grated nutmeg
150g/5oz/¾ cup cooked pitted
prunes, chopped

NUTRITION NOTES

Per portion
Energy	177Kcals/745kJ
Fat	4.6g
Saturated Fat	0.6g
Cholesterol	16mg
Fibre	1.5g

1 Preheat the oven to 200°C/400°F/ Gas 6. Grease a 12-cup muffin tin (pan) or use paper cases.

2 Break the egg into a mixing bowl and beat with a fork. Beat in the milk and oil. Stir in the sugars. Set aside.

3 Sift the flour, baking powder, salt and nutmeg into a mixing bowl. Make a well in the centre, pour in the egg mixture and stir until moistened. Do not overmix; the batter should be slightly lumpy.

4 Fold in the prunes.

5 Fill the prepared cups two-thirds full. Bake until golden brown, about 20 minutes. Leave to stand for 10 minutes before unmoulding. Serve warm or at room temperature.

Yogurt Honey Muffins

Serve with low-fat yogurt and a drizzle of honey for a delicious treat.

1 Preheat the oven to 190°C/375°F/ Gas 5. Grease a 12-cup muffin tin (pan) or use paper cases.

2 In a pan, melt the butter and honey. Remove from the heat and set aside to cool slightly.

3 In a bowl, whisk together the yogurt, egg, lemon rind and juice.

4 In another bowl, sift together the dry ingredients.

5 Stir the butter and honey into the yogurt mixture, then fold in the dry ingredients until just blended.

6 Fill the prepared cups two-thirds full. Bake for 20–25 minutes, until well risen and firm in the middle. Leave to cool in the tin for 5 minutes before unmoulding. Serve warm or at room temperature.

Makes 12
60ml/4 tbsp butter
75ml/5 tbsp thin honey
225g/8oz/1 cup natural (plain) yogurt
1 large (US extra large) egg
grated rind of 1 lemon
50ml/2fl oz/¼ cup fresh lemon juice
115g/4oz/1 cup plain (all-purpose) flour
115g/4oz/1 cup plain (all-purpose) wholemeal (whole-wheat) flour
7.5ml/1½ tsp bicarbonate soda (baking soda)
0.75ml/⅛ tsp freshly grated nutmeg

NUTRITION NOTES
Per portion
Energy	131Kcals/551kJ
Fat	4.1g
Saturated Fat	0.9g
Cholesterol	13mg
Fibre	1.7g

Variation

For Walnut Yogurt Honey Muffins, add 50g/2oz/½ cup chopped walnuts, folding in with the flour. This makes a more substantial muffin.

Blackberry, Sloe Gin and Rose Water Muffins

Bring a taste of the countryside to tea time with tantalising hedgerow fruits and delicate rose water.

Makes 12
300g/11oz/2⅔ cups plain (all-purpose) flour
50g/2oz/generous ¼ cup soft light brown sugar
60ml/4 tsp baking powder
pinch of salt
60g/2¼oz/generous ½ cup chopped blanched almonds
90g/3½oz/generous 1 cup fresh blackberries
2 eggs
200ml/7fl oz/scant 1 cup milk
60ml/4 tbsp melted butter
15ml/1 tbsp sloe gin
15ml/1 tbsp rose water

NUTRITION NOTES
Per portion

Energy	194Kcals/813kJ
Fat	8.1g
Saturated Fat	1.32g
Cholesterol	32.8mg
Fibre	1.4g

1 Preheat the oven to 200°C/400°F/ Gas 6. Grease a 12-cup muffin tin (pan) or use paper cases. Mix the flour, sugar, baking powder and salt in a bowl and stir in the almonds and blackberries, mixing them well to coat with the flour mixture.

2 In another bowl, mix the eggs with the milk, then gradually add the butter, sloe gin and rose water. Make a well in the centre of the bowl of dry ingredients and add the egg and milk mixture. Stir well.

3 Spoon the mixture into the greased muffin tin or paper cases. Bake for 20–25 minutes or until browned. Turn out the muffins on to a wire rack to cool. Serve with butter.

Date and Apple Muffins

You will only need one or two of these wholesome muffins per person, as they are very filling.

1 Preheat the oven to 200°C/400°F/ Gas 6. Grease a 12-cup muffin tin (pan) or use paper cases. Put the wholemeal flour in a mixing bowl. Sift in the white flour with the cinnamon and baking powder. Rub in the margarine until the mixture resembles breadcrumbs, then stir in the muscovado sugar.

4 Sprinkle with the chopped pecan nuts. Bake the muffins for 20–25 minutes until golden brown and firm in the middle. Transfer to a wire rack and serve while still warm.

Variation

Use a pear in place of the eating apple and chopped ready-to-eat dried apricots in place of the dates. Mixed (apple pie) spice is a good alternative to cinnamon.

Makes 12

150g/5oz/1¼ cups self-raising (self-rising) wholemeal (whole-wheat) flour
150g/5oz/1¼ cups self-raising (self-rising) white flour
5ml/1 tsp ground cinnamon
5ml/1 tsp baking powder
25g/1oz/2 tbsp soft margarine
75g/3oz/scant ½ cup light muscovado (brown) sugar
1 eating apple
250ml/8fl oz/1 cup apple juice
30ml/2 tbsp pear and apple spread
1 egg, lightly beaten
75g/3oz/½ cup chopped dates
15ml/1 tbsp chopped pecan nuts

NUTRITION NOTES

Per portion	
Energy	163Kcals/686kJ
Fat	2.98g
Saturated Fat	0.47g
Cholesterol	16.04mg
Fibre	1.97g

2 Quarter and core the apple, chop the flesh finely and set aside. Stir a little of the apple juice with the pear and apple spread until smooth. Mix in the remaining juice, then add to the rubbed-in dry ingredients with the egg. Add the chopped apple to the bowl with the dates. Mix quickly until just combined.

3 Divide the mixture evenly among the muffin cases.

Cherry Marmalade Muffins

Serve with marmalade for a tasty breakfast.

Makes 12

225g/8oz/2 cups self-raising
(self-rising) flour
5ml/1 tsp mixed (apple pie) spice
75g/3oz/6 tbsp caster (superfine) sugar
115g/4oz/½ cup glacé (candied)
cherries, quartered
30ml/2 tbsp orange marmalade
150ml/¼ pint/⅔ cup skimmed milk
50g/2oz/¼ cup soft
sunflower margarine
marmalade, to brush

NUTRITION NOTES

Per portion

Energy	154Kcals/650kJ
Fat	3.66g
Saturated Fat	0.68g
Cholesterol	0.54mg
Fibre	0.69g

1 Preheat the oven to 200°C/400°F/ Gas 6. Lightly grease a 12-cup muffin tin (pan) or use paper cases.

2 Sift together the flour and spice, then stir in the sugar and cherries.

3 Mix the marmalade with the milk and beat into the dry ingredients with the margarine. Spoon into the greased tins. Bake for 20–25 minutes, until golden brown and firm in the middle.

4 Turn out on to a wire rack and brush the tops with warmed marmalade. Serve warm or cold.

Fruit Salad Slices

Try these delicious fruit salad slices as an alternative to a traditional fruit cake.

1 Soak the dried fruits in the tea for several hours, or overnight. Drain and reserve the liquid.

2 Preheat the oven to 180°C/350°F/ Gas 4. Grease an 18cm/7in round cake tin (pan) and line the base with baking parchment.

3 Sift the flour into a bowl with the nutmeg. Stir in the muscovado sugar, fruit and tea. Add the oil and milk and mix well.

4 Spoon the mixture into the prepared tin and sprinkle with demerara sugar. Bake for 50–55 minutes or until firm. Turn out and cool on a wire rack. Cut into slices.

Serves 8

175g/6oz/1 cup roughly chopped dried fruit salad mixture, such as apples, apricots, prunes and peaches
250ml/8fl oz/1 cup hot black tea
225g/8oz/2 cups self-raising (self-rising) wholemeal (whole-wheat) flour
5ml/1 tsp freshly grated nutmeg
50g/2oz/4 tbsp dark muscovado (molasses) sugar
45ml/3 tbsp sunflower oil
45ml/3 tbsp skimmed milk
demerara (raw) sugar, to sprinkle

NUTRITION NOTES
Per portion

Energy	201Kcals/848kJ
Fat	4.99g
Saturated Fat	0.65g
Cholesterol	0.1mg
Fibre	3.89g

Pineapple and Cinnamon Drop Scones

Making the batter with pineapple juice instead of milk cuts down on fat and adds to the taste.

Makes 24

115g/4oz/1 cup self-raising (self-rising)
wholemeal (whole-wheat) flour
115g/4oz/1 cup self-raising (self-rising)
white flour
5ml/1 tsp ground cinnamon
15ml/1 tbsp caster (superfine) sugar
1 egg, beaten
300ml/½ pint/1¼ cups pineapple juice
75g/3oz/½ cup semi-dried
pineapple, chopped
oil, for greasing

NUTRITION NOTES

Per portion	
Energy	51Kcals/215kJ
Fat	0.81g
Saturated Fat	0.14g
Cholesterol	8.02mg
Fibre	0.76g

1 Preheat a griddle, heavy frying pan or an electric frying pan. Put the wholemeal flour in a mixing bowl. Sift in the white flour, add the cinnamon and sugar and make a well in the centre.

2 Add the egg with half the pineapple juice and gradually incorporate the surrounding flour to make a smooth batter. Beat in the remaining juice with the chopped pineapple.

3 Lightly grease the griddle or pan. Drop tablespoons of the batter on to the surface, leaving them until they bubble and the bubbles begin to burst.

4 Turn the drop scones with a palette knife (metal spatula) and cook until the underside is golden brown. Keep the cooked scones warm and moist by wrapping them in a clean napkin while continuing to cook successive batches.

Drop Scones

These little scones are delicious spread with jam.

Makes 18
225g/8oz/2 cups self-raising
(self-rising) flour
2.5ml/½ tsp salt
15ml/1 tbsp caster (superfine) sugar
1 egg, beaten
300ml/½ pint/1¼ cups skimmed milk
oil, for greasing

NUTRITION NOTES
Per portion
Energy	64Kcals/270kJ
Fat	1.09g
Saturated Fat	0.2g
Cholesterol	11.04mg
Fibre	0.43g

1 Preheat a griddle, heavy frying pan or an electric frying pan. Sift the flour and salt into a mixing bowl. Stir in the sugar and make a well in the centre.

4 Turn the drop scones over with a palette knife (metal spatula) and cook until the underside is golden brown. Keep the cooked drop scones warm and moist by wrapping them in a clean napkin while cooking successive batches.

2 Add the egg and half the milk, then gradually incorporate the surrounding flour to make a smooth batter. Beat in the remaining milk.

3 Lightly oil the griddle or pan. Drop tablespoons of the batter on to the surface, leaving them until they bubble and the bubbles begin to burst.

Variation
For savoury scones, add 2 chopped spring onions (scallions) and 15ml/ 1 tbsp freshly grated Parmesan cheese. Serve with cottage cheese.

Wholemeal Scones

Made with a mixture of flours, these scones are a high fibre, healthy alternative.

Makes 16

175g/6oz/¾ cup cold butter
225g/8oz/2 cups plain (all-purpose) wholemeal (whole-wheat) flour
175g/6oz/1 cup plain white flour
30ml/2 tbsp caster (superfine) sugar
2.5ml/½ tsp salt
12.5ml/2½ tsp bicarbonate of soda
2 eggs
175ml/6fl oz/¾ cup buttermilk
25g/1oz/¼ cup raisins

NUTRITION NOTES

Per portion

Energy	197Kcals/826kJ
Fat	9.8g
Saturated Fat	2g
Cholesterol	25mg
Fibre	2g

1 Preheat the oven to 200°C/400°F/ Gas 6. Grease and flour a large baking sheet.

2 Cut the butter into small pieces with a blunt knife.

3 Combine the dry ingredients in a bowl. Add the butter and cut in with a pastry blender until the mixture resembles coarse crumbs. Set aside.

4 In another bowl, whisk together the eggs and buttermilk. Set aside 30ml/2 tbsp for glazing.

5 Stir the remaining egg mixture into the dry ingredients until it just holds together. Stir in the raisins.

6 Roll out the dough about 2cm/¾in thick. Stamp out rounds with a cutter. Place on the prepared sheet and brush with the reserved glaze.

7 Bake in the preheated oven for 12–15 minutes, until golden. Allow to cool slightly before serving.

Orange Raisin Scones

A tang of orange gives these scones a special flavour.

1 Preheat the oven to 220°C/425°F/ Gas 7. Grease and flour a large baking sheet.

2 Combine the dry ingredients in a large bowl. Add the butter and margarine and cut in with a pastry blender until the mixture resembles coarse crumbs.

3 Add the orange rind and raisins. Gradually stir in the buttermilk to form a soft dough.

4 Roll out the dough about 2cm/¾in thick. Stamp out rounds with a cutter.

5 Place on the prepared sheet and brush the tops with milk. Bake for about 12–15 minutes, until golden. Serve hot or warm.

Makes 16

225g/8oz/2 cups plain (all-purpose) flour
25ml/1½ tbsp baking powder
75g/3oz/6 tbsp caster (superfine) sugar
2.5ml/½ tsp salt
75ml/5 tbsp butter, diced
75ml/5 tbsp margarine, diced
grated rind of 1 large orange
50g/2oz/⅓ cup raisins
115g/4oz/½ cup buttermilk
milk, for glazing

NUTRITION NOTES

Per portion

Energy	164Kcals/687kJ
Fat	7.9g
Saturated Fat	1.6g
Cholesterol	1mg
Fibre	0.7g

Cook's Tip

For light tender scones, handle the dough as little as possible. If you wish, split the scones when cool and toast them under a preheated grill. Butter them while still hot.

Sunflower Scones

Add a bit of crunch to your scones with this combination of sunflower seeds and sultanas.

Makes 10–12

225g/8oz/2 cups self-raising
(self-rising) flour
5ml/1 tsp baking powder
25g/1oz/2 tbsp soft sunflower margarine
25g/1oz/2 tbsp caster (superfine) sugar
50g/2oz/⅓ cup sultanas (golden raisins)
30ml/2 tbsp sunflower seeds
150g/5oz/⅔ cup natural (plain) yogurt
about 30–45ml/2–3 tbsp skimmed milk

NUTRITION NOTES

Per portion	
Energy	176Kcals/742kJ
Fat	5.32g
Saturated Fat	0.81g
Cholesterol	0.84mg
Fibre	1.26g

1 Preheat the oven to 230°C/450°F/
Gas 8. Lightly oil a baking sheet. Sift
the flour and baking powder into a bowl
and rub in the margarine evenly.

2 Stir in the sugar, sultanas and half the
sunflower seeds, then mix in the
yogurt, with just enough milk to make a
fairly soft, but not sticky dough.

3 Roll out on a lightly floured surface
to about 2cm/¾in thickness. Cut
into 6cm/2½in flower shapes or rounds
with a pastry (cookie) cutter and lift on to
the baking sheet.

4 Brush with milk and sprinkle with the
reserved sunflower seeds, then bake
for 10–12 minutes, until well risen and
golden brown.

5 Cool the scones on a wire rack.
Serve split and spread with jam or
low-fat spread.

Prune and Peel Rock Buns

Split these buns and serve with fromage frais or ricotta cheese, if you like.

Makes 12

225g/8oz/2 cups plain (all-purpose) flour
10ml/2 tsp baking powder
75g/3oz/⅓ cup demerara (raw) sugar
50g/2oz/¼ cup chopped ready-to-eat dried prunes
50g/2oz/⅓ cup chopped mixed peel
finely grated rind of 1 lemon
50ml/2fl oz/¼ cup sunflower oil
75ml/5 tbsp skimmed milk

1 Preheat the oven to 200°C/400°F/ Gas 6. Lightly oil a large baking sheet. Sift together the flour and baking powder, then stir in the sugar, prunes, peel and lemon rind.

2 Mix the oil and milk, then stir into the mixture, to make a dough that just binds together.

3 Spoon into rocky heaps on the baking sheet and bake for 20 minutes, until golden. Cool on a wire rack.

NUTRITION NOTES

Per portion

Energy	135Kcals/570kJ
Fat	3.35g
Saturated Fat	0.44g
Cholesterol	0.13mg
Fibre	0.86g

Banana and Apricot Chelsea Buns

These buns are old favourites given a low-fat twist with a delectable fruit filling.

Serves 9

about 90ml/6 tbsp warm skimmed milk
5ml/1 tsp dried yeast
pinch of sugar
225g/8oz/2 cups strong white
bread flour
10ml/2 tsp mixed (apple pie) spice
2.5ml/½ tsp salt
50g/2oz/¼ cup caster (superfine) sugar
25g/1oz/2 tbsp soft margarine
1 egg

For the filling

1 large ripe banana
175g/6oz/1 cup ready-to-eat
dried apricots
30ml/2 tbsp caster (superfine) sugar
30ml/2 tbsp light muscovado
(brown) sugar

For the glaze

30ml/2 tbsp caster (superfine) sugar
30ml/2 tbsp water

Cook's Tip

Do not leave the buns in the tin
for too long or the glaze will
stick to the sides, making them
very difficult to remove.

NUTRITION NOTES

Per portion

Energy	214Kcals/901kJ
Fat	2.18g
Saturated Fat	0.63g
Cholesterol	21.59mg
Fibre	2.18g

1 Lightly grease an 18cm/7in square
tin. Put the warm milk in a jug and
sprinkle the yeast on top. Add a pinch of
sugar to help activate the yeast, mix well
and leave for 30 minutes.

2 Sift the flour, spice and salt into a
mixing bowl. Stir in the caster sugar,
rub in the margarine, then stir in the
yeast mixture and the egg. Gradually mix
in the flour to make a soft dough, adding
extra milk if needed.

3 Turn out the dough on to a floured
surface and knead for 5 minutes until
smooth and elastic. Return the dough to
the clean bowl, cover with a damp tea
towel and leave in a warm place for about
2 hours, until doubled in bulk.

4 To prepare the filling, mash the
banana in a bowl. Using scissors,
snip the apricots into pieces, then stir
into the banana with the sugars.

5 Knead the dough on a floured surface
for 2 minutes, then roll out to a
30 x 23cm/12 x 9in rectangle. Spread the
banana and apricot filling over the dough
and roll up lengthways like a Swiss (jelly)
roll, with the join underneath.

6 Cut the roll into nine buns. Place, cut
side down, in the tin, cover and leave
to rise for 30 minutes. Preheat the oven
to 200°C/400°F/Gas 6 and bake for 20–
25 minutes. Meanwhile, mix the caster
sugar and water in a small pan. Heat,
stirring, until dissolved, then boil for
2 minutes. Brush the glaze over the
cooked buns while still hot.

Blueberry Streusel Slice

This soft berry filling tastes delicious with the nutty topping.

Makes about 30 slices

225g/8oz shortcrust pastry,
thawed if frozen
50g/2oz/½ cup plain (all-purpose) flour
1.5ml/¼ tsp baking powder
40g/1½oz/3 tbsp butter or margarine
50g/2oz/¼ cup soft light brown sugar
25g/1oz/½ cup fresh white breadcrumbs
1.5ml/¼ tsp salt
50g/2oz/½ cup flaked (sliced) or
chopped almonds
30ml/4 tbsp blackberry or bramble jelly
115g/4oz/1 cup blueberries

NUTRITION NOTES

Per portion

Energy	77Kcals/322kJ
Fat	4.16g
Saturated Fat	1.57g
Cholesterol	5.84mg
Fibre	0.95g

1 Preheat the oven to 180°F/350°F/ Gas 4. Roll out the pastry on a lightly floured surface to line an 18 x 28cm/ 7 x 11in Swiss roll tin (jelly roll pan). Prick the base evenly with a fork.

2 Rub together the flour, baking powder, butter or margarine, sugar, breadcrumbs and salt until crumbly, then mix in the almonds.

3 Spread the pastry with the jelly, sprinkle with the blueberries, then cover evenly with the almond mixture, pressing down lightly. Bake for 20 minutes, then reduce the temperature to 160°C/325°F/Gas 3 and cook for a further 10–20 minutes.

4 Remove from the oven when golden on the top and the pastry is cooked through. Cut into slices while still hot, then allow to cool.

Sticky Date and Apple Bars

If possible, allow this mixture to mature for 1–2 days before cutting – it will get stickier and better!

Makes about 16 bars

115g/4oz/½ cup margarine
50g/2oz/¼ cup soft dark brown sugar
50g/2oz/4 tbsp golden (light corn) syrup
115g/4oz/¾ cup chopped dates
115g/4oz/generous 1 cup rolled oats
115g/4oz/1 cup self-raising (self-rising)
wholemeal (whole-wheat) flour
225g/8oz eating apples, peeled, cored
and grated, and sprinkled with 5–10ml/
1–2 tsp lemon juice
20–25 walnut halves

1 Preheat the oven to 190°C/375°F/
Gas 5. Line an 18–20cm/7–8in square
or rectangular loose-based cake tin (pan).
In a large pan, heat the margarine, sugar,
syrup and dates, stirring until the dates
soften completely.

2 Gradually work in the oats, flour and
apples until well mixed. Spoon into
the tin and spread out evenly. Top with
the walnut halves.

3 Bake for 30 minutes, then reduce the
temperature to 160°C/325°F/Gas 3
and bake for 10–20 minutes more, until
firm to the touch and golden. Cut into
squares or bars while still warm, and
keep for 1–2 days before eating.

NUTRITION NOTES

Per portion

Energy	183Kcals/763kJ
Fat	10.11g
Saturated Fat	1.64g
Cholesterol	0.14mg
Fibre	1g

Apricot Sponge Bars

These fingers are delicious at tea time – the apricots keep them moist for several days.

Makes 18

225g/8oz/2 cups self-raising
(self-rising) flour
115g/4oz/½ cup soft light brown sugar
50g/2oz/⅓ cup semolina
175g/6oz/¾ cup ready-to-eat dried
apricots, chopped
30ml/2 tbsp clear honey
30ml/2 tbsp malt extract
2 eggs
60ml/4 tbsp skimmed milk
60ml/4 tbsp sunflower oil
a few drops of almond essence (extract)
30ml/2 tbsp flaked (sliced) almonds

NUTRITION NOTES

Per portion	
Energy	153Kcals/641kJ
Fat	4.5g
Saturated Fat	0.61g
Cholesterol	21.5mg
Fibre	1.27g

1 Preheat the oven to 160°C/325°F/ Gas 3. Lightly grease and then line an 18 x 28cm/7 x 11in baking tin (pan).

2 Sift the flour into a bowl and mix in the sugar, semolina and apricots. Make a well in the centre and add the honey, malt extract, eggs, milk, oil and almond essence. Mix the ingredients together thoroughly until smooth.

3 Spoon the mixture into the tin, spreading it to the edges, then sprinkle over the flaked almonds.

4 Bake for 30–35 minutes, or until the centre springs back when lightly pressed. Remove from the tin and turn on to a wire rack to cool. Cut into 18 slices using a sharp knife.

Cook's Tip

If you can't find pre-soaked apricots, use chopped ordinary dried apricots soaked in boiling water for 1 hour, then drain and add to the mixture.

Apricot Yogurt Cookies

These soft cookies are very quick to make and are useful for lunch boxes.

1 Preheat the oven to 190°C/375°F/ Gas 5. Lightly oil a large baking sheet.

2 Sift together the flour, baking powder and cinnamon. Stir in the oats, sugar, apricots and nuts.

3 Beat together the yogurt and oil, then stir evenly into the mixture to make a firm dough. If necessary, add a little more yogurt.

4 Use your hands to roll the mixture into about 16 small balls, place on the baking sheet and flatten with a fork.

5 Sprinkle with demerara sugar. Bake the cookies for 15–20 minutes, or until firm and golden brown. Leave to cool on a wire rack.

Makes 16

175g/6oz/1½ cups plain (all-purpose) flour
5ml/1 tsp baking powder
5ml/1 tsp ground cinnamon
75g/3oz/scant 1 cup rolled oats
75g/3oz/⅓ cup light muscovado (brown) sugar
115g/4oz/½ cup chopped ready-to-eat dried apricots
15ml/1 tbsp flaked (sliced) hazelnuts or almonds
about 150g/5oz/⅔ cup natural (plain) yogurt
45ml/3 tbsp sunflower oil
demerara (raw) sugar, to sprinkle

NUTRITION NOTES

Per portion

Energy	95Kcals/400kJ
Fat	2.66g
Saturated Fat	0.37g
Cholesterol	0.3mg
Fibre	0.94g

Cook's Tip

These cookies do not keep well, so it is best to eat them within two days, or to freeze them. Pack into polythene bags and freeze for up to four months.

Buttermilk Cookies

Low in fat, these biscuits are perfect for a mid-morning snack.

Makes 15

75g/6oz/1½ cups plain (all-purpose) flour
5ml/1 tsp salt
5ml/1 tsp baking powder
2.5ml/½ tsp bicarbonate of soda (baking soda)
60ml/4 tbsp cold butter or margarine
175ml/6fl oz/¾ cup buttermilk

NUTRITION NOTES

Per portion	
Energy	85Kcals/359kJ
Fat	3.5g
Saturated Fat	0.7g
Cholesterol	0.5mg
Fibre	0.5g

1 Preheat the oven to 220°C/425°F/ Gas 7. Grease a baking sheet. Sift the dry ingredients into a bowl. Cut in the butter or margarine with a pastry blender until the mixture resembles coarse crumbs.

2 Gradually pour in the buttermilk, stirring with a fork to form a soft dough.

3 Roll out the biscuit dough to about a 1cm/½in thickness.

4 Stamp out 5cm/2in rounds with a pastry (cookie) cutter. Place on the prepared tray and bake for 12–15 minutes, or until golden. Serve warm or at room temperature.

Shortcake

Delicious served warm with a low-fat spread.

1 Preheat the oven to 220°C/425°F/ Gas 7. Grease a baking sheet.

2 Sift the flour, sugar, baking powder and salt into a bowl.

3 Cut in the butter with a pastry blender until the mixture resembles coarse crumbs.

4 Pour in the milk and stir with a fork to form a soft dough.

5 Roll out the dough to about 5mm/¼in thickness. Stamp out rounds with a 6cm/2½in pastry (cookie) cutter. Place on the prepared sheet and bake for about 12 minutes, or until golden. Serve hot or warm.

Makes 8

165g/5½oz/1⅓ cups plain (all-purpose) flour
30ml/2 tbsp caster (superfine) sugar
15ml/1 tbsp baking powder
0.75ml/⅛ tsp salt
75ml/5 tbsp cold butter, cut in pieces
120ml/4fl oz/½ cup skimmed milk

NUTRITION NOTES

Per portion
Energy	176Kcals/740kJ
Fat	8g
Saturated Fat	1.5g
Cholesterol	1mg
Fibre	0.8g

Variation

For Berry Shortcake, split the biscuits in half while still warm. Top one half with lightly sugared fresh berries such as strawberries, raspberries or blueberries, and sandwich with the other half. Serve with dollops of thick, low-fat yogurt.

Oaty Crisps

These cookies are very crisp and crunchy – ideal to serve with morning coffee.

Makes 18

175g/6oz/1½ cups rolled oats
75g/3oz/⅓ cup light muscovado (brown) sugar
1 egg
60ml/4 tbsp sunflower oil
30ml/2 tbsp malt extract

NUTRITION NOTES

Per portion	
Energy	86Kcals/360kJ
Fat	3.59g
Saturated Fat	0.57g
Cholesterol	10.7mg
Fibre	0.66g

1 Preheat the oven to 190°C/375°F/ Gas 5. Lightly grease two baking sheets. Mix the rolled oats and sugar in a bowl, breaking up any lumps in the sugar. Add the egg, sunflower oil and malt extract, mix well, then leave to soak for 15 minutes.

2 Using a teaspoon, place small heaps of the mixture well apart on the prepared baking sheets. Press the heaps into 7.5cm/3in rounds with the back of a dampened fork.

3 Bake the cookies for 10–15 minutes until golden brown. Leave them to cool for 1 minute, then remove with a palette knife (metal spatula) and cool on a wire rack.

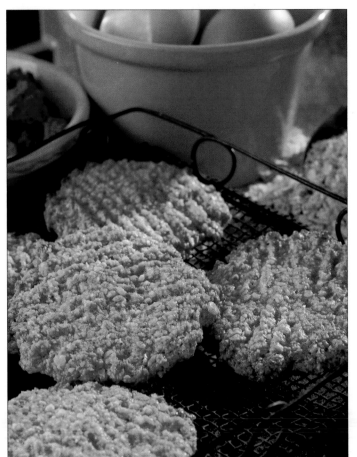

Cook's Tip

To give these biscuits a coarser texture, substitute jumbo oats for some or all of the rolled oats. Once cool, store the biscuits in an airtight container to keep them as crisp and fresh as possible.

Orange Cookies

A popular choice for a well-earned coffee break.

Makes 30
115g/4oz/½ cup butter
200g/7oz/1 cup caster (superfine) sugar
2 egg yolks
15ml/1 tbsp fresh orange juice
grated rind of 1 orange
175g/6oz/1½ cups plain
(all-purpose) flour
115g/4oz/½ cup self-raising
(self-rising) flour
2.5ml/½ tsp salt
5ml/1 tsp baking powder

1 With an electric mixer, cream the butter and sugar until light and fluffy. Add the yolks, orange juice and rind, and continue beating to blend. Set aside.

6 Press down with a fork to flatten. Bake for 8–10 minutes, until golden brown. With a metal spatula, transfer to a rack to cool.

NUTRITION NOTES
Per portion

Energy	84Kcals/353kJ
Fat	3.5g
Saturated Fat	0.7g
Cholesterol	14mg
Fibre	0.2g

2 In another bowl, sift together the flours, salt and baking powder. Add to the butter mixture and stir until it forms a dough.

3 Wrap the dough in baking parchment and chill for 2 hours.

4 Preheat the oven to 190°C/375°F/ Gas 5. Grease two baking sheets.

5 Roll spoonfuls of the dough into balls and place 2.5–5cm/1–2in apart on the prepared sheets.

Breads

The aroma of freshly-
baked bread makes
every house feel like a
home. And these low-fat
loaves also taste
tantalizingly good.

White Bread

The classic white loaf, perfect for breakfast toast.

Makes 2 loaves

50ml/2fl oz/¼ cup lukewarm water
10ml/2 tsp dried yeast
30ml/2 tbsp caster (superfine) sugar
475ml/16fl oz/2 cups lukewarm
skimmed milk
30ml/2 tbsp butter or margarine
10ml/2 tsp salt
675–800g/1½–1¾lb/6–7 cups
strong white bread flour

NUTRITION NOTES

Per portion (serves 12)

Energy	178Kcals/757kJ
Fat	1.8g
Saturated Fat	0.3g
Cholesterol	1mg
Fibre	1.4g

1 Combine the water, yeast and 15ml/ 1 tbsp sugar in a measuring cup and leave for 15 minutes.

2 Pour the milk into a large bowl. Add the remaining sugar, the butter or margarine, the salt and the yeast mixture.

3 Stir in the flour, 115g/4oz/1 cup at a time, until a stiff dough is formed. Alternatively, use a food processor.

4 Transfer the dough to a floured surface. To knead, push the dough away from you with the palm of your hand, then fold it towards you, and push it away again. Repeat until the dough is smooth and elastic.

5 Place the dough in a large greased bowl, cover with a plastic bag, and leave to rise in a warm place until doubled in volume, 2–3 hours. Grease two 23 x 13cm/9 x 5in loaf tins (pans).

6 Knock back (punch down) the risen dough with your fist and divide in half. Form into loaf shapes and place in the tins, seam-side down. Cover and leave to rise in a warm place until almost doubled in volume, about 45 minutes.

7 Preheat the oven to 190°C/375°F/ Gas 5. Bake for 45–50 minutes, until firm and brown. Unmould and tap the bottom of a loaf: if it sounds hollow, the loaf is done. If necessary, return to the oven and bake a few minutes more. Transfer to a rack to cool.

Country Bread

A wholemeal loaf that is high in fibre and low in fat.

Makes 2 loaves

275g/10oz/2½ cups strong wholemeal (whole-wheat) bread flour
275g/10oz/2½ cups plain (all-purpose) flour
115g/4oz/1 cup strong white bread flour
20ml/4 tsp salt
60ml/4 tbsp butter
475ml/16fl oz/2 cups lukewarm milk

For the starter

10ml/2 tsp dried yeast
250ml/8fl oz/1 cup lukewarm water
115g/4oz/1 cup plain (all-purpose) flour
1.5ml/¼ tsp caster (superfine) sugar

NUTRITION NOTES

Per portion (serves 12)

Energy	204Kcals/863kJ
Fat	3.3g
Saturated Fat	0.6g
Cholesterol	1mg
Fibre	2.7g

1 For the starter, combine the yeast, water, flour and sugar in a bowl and stir with a fork. Cover and leave in a warm place for 2–3 hours, or leave overnight in a cool place.

2 Place the flours, salt and butter in a food processor and process just until blended, for 1–2 minutes. Stir together the milk and starter, then slowly pour into the processor, with the motor running, until the mixture forms a dough. If necessary, add more water. Alternatively, the dough can be mixed by hand. Transfer to a floured surface and knead until smooth and elastic.

3 Place in an ungreased bowl, cover with a plastic bag, and leave to rise in a warm place until doubled in volume, for about 1½ hours. Transfer to a floured surface and knead briefly. Return to the bowl and leave to rise until tripled in volume, about 1½ hours.

5 For each loaf, top the large ball with the small ball and press the centre with the handle of a wooden spoon to secure. Cover with a plastic bag, slash the top, and leave to rise.

6 Preheat the oven to 200°C/400°F/ Gas 6. Dust the dough with wholemeal flour and bake for 45–50 minutes, until the top is browned and the bottom sounds hollow when tapped. Cool on a rack before serving.

4 Divide the dough in half. Cut off one-third of the dough from each half and shape into balls. Shape the larger remaining halves into balls. Grease a baking sheet.

Poppy Seed Rolls

Pile these soft rolls in a basket and serve them for breakfast or with dinner.

Makes 12

300ml/½ pint/1¼ cups warm skimmed milk
5ml/1 tsp dried yeast
pinch of sugar
450g/1lb/4 cups strong white bread flour
5ml/1 tsp salt
1 egg

For the topping
1 egg, beaten
poppy seeds

Cook's Tip

Use easy-blend (rapid rise) dried yeast if you prefer. Add it directly to the dry ingredients and mix with hand-hot milk. The rolls will only require one rising (see package instructions). Vary the toppings. Linseed, sesame seeds and caraway seeds are all good; try adding caraway seeds to the dough, too, for extra flavour.

NUTRITION NOTES

Per portion	
Energy	160Kcals/674kJ
Fat	2.42g
Saturated Fat	0.46g
Cholesterol	32.58mg
Fibre	1.16g

1 Put half the warm milk in a small bowl. Sprinkle the yeast on top. Add the sugar, mix well and leave to stand for 30 minutes.

2 Sift the flour and salt into a mixing bowl. Make a well in the centre and pour in the yeast mixture and the egg. Gradually incorporate the flour, adding enough of the remaining milk to mix to a soft dough.

3 Turn the dough on to a floured surface and knead for 5 minutes until smooth and elastic. Return to the clean bowl, cover with a damp dishtowel and leave in a warm place to rise for about 1 hour until doubled in bulk.

4 Lightly grease two baking sheets. Turn the dough on to a floured surface. Knead for 2 minutes, then cut into 12 pieces and shape into rolls.

5 Place the rolls on the prepared baking sheets, cover loosely with a large plastic bag (ballooning it to trap the air inside) and leave to stand in a warm place until the rolls have risen well. Preheat the oven to 220°C/425°F/Gas 7.

6 Glaze the rolls with the beaten egg, sprinkle with poppy seeds and bake for 12–15 minutes until golden brown. Transfer to a wire rack to cool.

Braided Loaf

An attractive, traditional loaf that would be fun as a dinner party accompaniment.

Makes 1 loaf

10ml/2 tsp dried yeast
5ml/1 tsp honey
250ml/8fl oz/1 cup lukewarm
skimmed milk
50g/2oz/¼ cup butter, melted
350g/12oz/3 cups strong white bread flour
5ml/1 tsp salt
1 egg, lightly beaten
1 egg yolk, beaten with 5ml/1 tsp
skimmed milk, for glazing

NUTRITION NOTES

Per portion (serves 10)

Energy	222Kcals/938kJ
Fat	6.6g
Saturated Fat	1.35g
Cholesterol	40.3mg
Fibre	1.4g

1 Combine the yeast, honey, milk and butter, stir, and leave for 15 minutes to dissolve.

2 In a large bowl, mix together the flour and salt. Make a well in the centre and add the yeast mixture and egg. With a wooden spoon, stir from the centre, incorporating flour with each turn, to obtain a rough dough.

3 Transfer to a floured surface and knead until smooth and elastic. Place in a clean bowl, cover, and leave to rise in a warm place until doubled in volume, for about 1½ hours.

4 Grease a baking sheet. Knock back (punch down) the dough and divide into three equal pieces. Roll to shape each piece into a long thin strip.

5 Begin braiding from the centre strip, tucking in the ends to conceal them. Cover loosely and leave to rise in a warm place for 30 minutes.

6 Preheat the oven to 190°C/375°F/ Gas 5. Place the bread in a cool place while the oven heats. Brush with the glaze and bake until golden, for 40–45 minutes. Set on a rack to cool completely before serving.

Sesame Seed Bread

Sesame seeds have a distinctive flavour as well as a crunchy texture.

1 Combine the yeast and 150ml/¼ pint/ ⅔ cup of the water and leave to dissolve. Mix the flours and salt in a large bowl. Make a well in the centre and pour in the yeast and the remaining water.

2 With a wooden spoon, stir from the centre, incorporating flour with each turn, to obtain a rough dough.

3 Transfer to a floured surface. To knead, push the dough away from you with the palm of your hand, then fold it towards you, and push away again. Repeat until smooth and elastic, then return to the bowl and cover with a plastic bag. Leave in a warm place until doubled in volume, for 1½–2 hours.

4 Grease a 23cm/9in cake tin. Knock back (punch down) the dough and knead in the sesame seeds. Divide the dough into 16 balls and place in the pan. Cover with a plastic bag and leave in a warm place until risen above the rim of the pan.

5 Preheat the oven to 220°C/425°F/ Gas 7. Brush the top of the loaf with milk and sprinkle with the sesame seeds. Bake for 15 minutes. Lower the heat to 190°C/375°F/Gas 5 and bake until the bottom sounds hollow when tapped, about 30 minutes more. Cool on a rack.

Makes 1 loaf
10ml/2 tsp dried yeast
350ml/12fl oz/1½ cups lukewarm water
175g/6oz/1½ cups strong white
bread flour
185g/6½oz/1⅔ cups strong wholemeal
(whole-wheat) bread flour
10ml/2 tsp salt
75g/3oz/¾ cup toasted sesame seeds
milk, for glazing
30ml/2 tbsp sesame seeds, for sprinkling

NUTRITION NOTES

Per portion (serves 10–12)
Energy	218Kcals/918kJ
Fat	7.5g
Saturated Fat	1.1g
Cholesterol	0
Fibre	3.6g

Parker House Rolls

These easy-to-make rolls are perfect if you're catering for large numbers.

Makes 48 rolls
10ml/2 tsp dried yeast
475ml/16fl oz/2 cups lukewarm skimmed milk
115g/4oz/½ cup margarine
75ml/5 tbsp caster (superfine) sugar
10ml/2 tsp salt
2 eggs
800–900g/1¾–2lb/7–8 cups strong white bread flour
50g/2oz/¼ cup butter

NUTRITION NOTES

Per portion
Energy	114Kcals/479kJ
Fat	3.5g
Saturated Fat	0.68g
Cholesterol	8.5mg
Fibre	0.7g

1 Combine the yeast and 120ml/4fl oz/ ½ cup of milk in a large bowl. Stir and leave for 15 minutes to dissolve. Bring the remaining milk to a simmer, cool for 5 minutes, then beat in the margarine, sugar, salt and eggs. Allow to cool to lukewarm.

2 Pour the milk mixture into the yeast mixture. Stir in 450g/1lb/4 cups of flour with a wooden spoon. Add the remaining flour, 225g/8oz/2 cups at a time, until a rough dough is obtained.

3 Transfer the dough to a lightly floured surface and knead until it is smooth and elastic. Place in a clean bowl, cover with a plastic bag, and leave to rise in a warm place until doubled in volume, for about 2 hours.

4 In a pan, melt the butter and set aside. Grease two baking sheets. Knock back (punch down) the dough and divide into four equal pieces. Roll each piece into a 20 x 30cm/8 x 12in rectangle, about 5mm/¼in thick.

5 Cut each of the rolled-out rectangular pieces into four 5 x 30cm/2 x 12in strips. Cut each strip into three 10 x 5cm/ 4 x 2in rectangles.

6 Brush each rectangle with melted butter, then fold the rectangles in half, so that the top extends about 1cm/½in over the bottom.

7 Place the rolls slightly overlapping on the baking sheet, with the longer side facing up.

8 Cover and chill for 30 minutes. Preheat the oven to 180°C/350°F/Gas 4. Bake until golden, for 18–20 minutes. Cool the rolls slightly before serving.

Clover Leaf Rolls

Create these clever rolls by baking them in a muffin tin.

Makes 24
300ml/½ pint/1¼ cups skimmed milk
10ml/2 tbsp caster (superfine) sugar
50g/2oz/¼ cup butter
10ml/2 tsp dried yeast
1 egg
10ml/2 tsp salt
350–450g/12oz–1lb/3–4 cups strong
white bread flour
melted butter, for glazing

NUTRITION NOTES
Per portion
Energy	109Kcals/459kJ
Fat	2.9g
Saturated Fat	0.6g
Cholesterol	8mg
Fibre	0.7g

1 Heat the milk until lukewarm; test the temperature with your knuckle. Pour into a large bowl and stir in the sugar, butter and yeast. Leave for 15 minutes.

2 Stir the egg and salt into the yeast mixture. Gradually stir in 350g/12oz/ 3 cups of the flour. Add just enough extra flour to obtain a rough dough.

5 Place three balls, side by side, in each muffin cup. Cover loosely and leave to rise in a warm place for about half an hour, until doubled in volume.

6 Preheat the oven to 200°C/400°F/ Gas 6. Brush with glaze. Bake for about 20 minutes, until lightly browned. Cool slightly before serving.

3 Knead on a floured surface until smooth and elastic. Place in a greased bowl, cover, and leave in a warm place until doubled in volume, for about 1½ hours. Grease two 12-cup muffin tins (pans).

4 Knock back (punch down) the dough. Cut into four equal pieces. Roll each piece into a rope 35cm/14in long. Cut each rope into 18 pieces, then roll each into a ball.

Wholemeal Buttermilk Rolls

These traditional wholemeal rolls are made with buttermilk to keep the fat content low.

Makes 12

10ml/2 tsp dried yeast
50ml/2fl oz/¼ cup lukewarm water
5ml/1 tsp caster (superfine) sugar
175ml/6fl oz/¾ cup lukewarm buttermilk
1.5ml/¼ tsp bicarbonate of soda
(baking soda)
5ml/1 tsp salt
40g/1½oz/3 tbsp butter
185g/6½oz/1⅔ cups strong wholemeal
(whole-wheat) bread flour
115g/4oz/1 cup strong white bread flour
1 beaten egg, for glazing

NUTRITION NOTES

Per portion	
Energy	143Kcals/603kJ
Fat	4.2g
Saturated Fat	0.8g
Cholesterol	17mg
Fibre	2.1g

1 In a large bowl, combine the yeast, water and sugar. Stir, and leave for 15 minutes to dissolve.

2 Add the buttermilk, bicarbonate of soda, salt and butter and stir to blend. Stir in the wholemeal flour.

3 Add just enough of the plain flour to obtain a rough dough. If the dough is stiff, stir it with your hands.

4 Transfer to a floured surface and knead until smooth and elastic. Divide into three equal parts. Roll each into a cylinder, then cut into four.

5 Form the pieces into torpedo shapes. Place on a greased baking sheet, cover, and leave in a warm place until doubled in volume.

6 Preheat the oven to 200°C/400°F/Gas 6. Brush with the glaze. Bake for 15–20 minutes, until firm. Allow to cool.

French Bread

A French stick is perfect for garlic bread or sandwiches.

1 Combine the yeast and water, stir, and leave for 15 minutes to dissolve. Stir in the salt.

2 Add the flour, 115g/4oz/1 cup at a time. Beat in with a wooden spoon, adding just enough flour for a smooth dough. Alternatively, use an electric mixer with a dough hook attachment.

3 Transfer to a floured surface and knead until smooth and elastic.

4 Shape into a ball, place in a greased bowl, and cover with a plastic bag. Leave to rise in a warm place until doubled in volume, for 2–4 hours.

6 Score the tops in several places with a very sharp knife. Brush with water and place in a cold oven. Set a pan of boiling water on the bottom of the oven and set the oven to 200°C/400°F/Gas 6. Bake until crusty and golden, for about 40 minutes. Cool on a rack.

Makes 2 loaves

10ml/2 tsp dried yeast
475ml/16fl oz/2 cups lukewarm water
5ml/1 tsp salt
675–900g/1½–2lb/6–8 cups strong white bread flour
corn meal, for sprinkling

NUTRITION NOTES

Per portion (serves 16)

Energy	96Kcals/411kJ
Fat	0.37g
Saturated Fat	0.13g
Cholesterol	0
Fibre	0.87g

5 Transfer to a lightly floured board, halve the dough and shape into two long loaves. Place on a baking sheet sprinkled with corn meal, and leave to rise for 5 minutes.

Buttermilk Graham Bread

If you can't find graham flour, wholemeal will make an equally delicious loaf.

Makes 8
10ml/2 tsp dried yeast
120ml/4fl oz/½ cup lukewarm water
225g/8oz/2 cups graham or strong
wholemeal (whole-wheat) bread flour
350g/12oz/3 cups strong white bread flour
130g/4½oz/generous 1 cup corn meal
10ml/2 tsp salt
30ml/2 tbsp caster (superfine) sugar
50g/2oz/¼ cup butter
475ml/16fl oz/2 cups
lukewarm buttermilk
1 beaten egg, for glazing
sesame seeds, for sprinkling

NUTRITION NOTES
Per portion
Energy	195Kcals/824kJ
Fat	4g
Saturated Fat	0.8g
Cholesterol	10mg
Fibre	1.9g

1 Combine the yeast and water, stir, and leave for 15 minutes to dissolve.

2 Mix together the graham or wholemeal flour, white flour, corn meal, salt and sugar in a large bowl. Make a well in the centre of the dry ingredients and pour in the yeast mixture, then add the butter and the buttermilk.

3 Stir from the centre, mixing in the flour until a rough dough is formed. If too stiff, use your hands.

4 Transfer to a floured surface and knead until smooth. Place in a clean bowl, cover, and leave in a warm place until doubled, for 2–3 hours.

5 Grease two 20cm/8in square baking tins (pans). Knock back (punch down) the dough. Divide into eight equal pieces and roll the pieces into balls. Place four balls in each tin. Cover and leave in a warm place until the dough rises above the rim of the tins, about 1 hour.

6 Preheat the oven to 190°C/375°F/Gas 5. Brush with the glaze, then sprinkle over the sesame seeds. Bake for about 40 minutes, or until the bottoms sound hollow when tapped. Leave to cool on a wire rack.

Multigrain Bread

Try replacing the wheatgerm or soy flour with rye, barley or buckwheat.

1 Combine the yeast and water, stir, and leave for 15 minutes to dissolve.

2 Place the rolled oats in a large bowl. Heat the milk until scalded, then pour over the oats.

3 Stir in the salt, oil, sugar and honey. Cool the mixture to 29°C/85°F.

4 Stir in the yeast mixture, eggs, wheatgerm, soy and wholemeal flours. Gradually stir in enough white flour to obtain a rough dough.

5 Transfer the dough to a floured surface and knead, adding flour if necessary, until smooth and elastic. Return to a clean bowl, cover, and leave to rise in a warm place until doubled in volume, for about 2–2½ hours.

6 Grease two 20 x 10cm/8 x 4in bread tins (pans). Knock back (punch down) the risen dough with your fist and knead briefly.

7 Divide the dough into quarters. Roll each quarter into a cylinder 4cm/1½in thick. Twist together two cylinders and place in a tin; repeat for remaining cylinders.

8 Cover and leave to rise until doubled in size, about 1 hour.

9 Preheat the oven to 190°C/375°F/Gas 5.

10 Bake the loaves for about 45–50 minutes in the centre of the oven, until the bottoms sound hollow when tapped lightly. Remove from the tins and allow to cool on a rack.

Makes 2 loaves

10ml/2 tsp dried yeast
50ml/2fl oz/¼ cup lukewarm water
75g/3oz/scant 1 cup rolled oats
475ml/16fl oz/2 cups skimmed milk
10ml/2 tsp salt
50ml/2fl oz/¼ cup oil
50g/2oz/¼ cup soft brown sugar
30ml/2 tbsp clear honey
2 eggs, lightly beaten
75g/3oz/½ cup wheatgerm
115g/4oz/1 cup soy flour
225g/8oz/2 cups strong wholemeal (whole-wheat) bread flour
350–400g/12–14oz/3–3½ cups strong white bread flour

NUTRITION NOTES

Per portion (serves 12)

Energy	238Kcals/1007kJ
Fat	4.4g
Saturated Fat	0.64g
Cholesterol	19.7mg
Fibre	4.2g

Austrian Three Grain Bread

A mixture of grains gives this close-textured bread a delightful nutty flavour.
Make two smaller twists, if preferred.

Makes 1 loaf
475ml/16fl oz/2 cups warm water
10ml/2 tsp dried yeast
pinch of sugar
225g/8oz/2 cups strong white
bread flour
7.5ml/1½ tsp salt
225g/8oz/2 cups malted brown flour
225g/8oz/2 cups rye flour
30ml/2 tbsp linseed
75g/3oz/¾ cup medium oatmeal
45ml/3 tbsp sunflower seeds
30ml/2 tbsp malt extract

1 Put half the water in a jug. Sprinkle the yeast on top. Add the sugar, mix well and leave for 10 minutes.

5 Grease a baking sheet. Turn the dough on to a floured surface, knead for 2 minutes, then divide in half. Roll each half into a 30cm/12in long sausage.

2 Sift the white flour and salt into a mixing bowl and add the other flours. Set aside 5ml/1 tsp of the linseed and add the rest to the flour mixture with the oatmeal and sunflower seeds. Make a well in the centre. Add the yeast mixture to the bowl with the malt extract and the remaining water.

3 Gradually incorporate the flour.

6 Twist the two sausages together, dampen the ends and press to seal. Lift the twist on to the prepared baking sheet. Brush the plait with water, sprinkle with the remaining linseed and cover loosely with a large plastic bag (ballooning it to trap the air inside). Leave in a warm place until well risen. Preheat the oven to 220°C/425°F/Gas 7.

NUTRITION NOTES

Per portion (serves 8–10)
Energy	367Kcals/1540kJ
Fat	5.36g
Saturated Fat	0.6g
Cholesterol	0
Fibre	6.67g

4 Mix to a soft dough, adding extra water if necessary. Turn out on to a floured surface and knead for about 5 minutes until smooth and elastic. Return to the clean bowl, cover with a damp dishtowel and leave to rise for about 2 hours until doubled in bulk.

7 Bake the loaf for 10 minutes, then lower the oven temperature to 200°C/400°F/Gas 6 and cook for 20 minutes more, or until the loaf sounds hollow when it is tapped underneath. Transfer to a wire rack to cool.

Granary Baps

These make excellent picnic fare, filled with cottage cheese, tuna, salad and low-fat mayonnaise.
They are also very good served warm with soup.

Makes 8
300ml/½ pint/1¼ cups warm water
5ml/1 tsp dried yeast
pinch of sugar
450g/1lb/4 cups malted brown
bread flour
5ml/1 tsp salt
15ml/1 tbsp malt extract
15ml/1 tbsp rolled oats

1 Put half the warm water in a jug. Sprinkle in the yeast. Add the sugar, mix well and leave for 10 minutes.

2 Put the malted brown flour and salt in a mixing bowl and make a well in the centre. Add the yeast mixture with the malt extract and the remaining water. Gradually incorporate the flour and mix to a soft dough.

3 Turn the dough on to a floured surface and knead for 5 minutes until smooth and elastic. Return to the clean bowl, cover with a damp dishtowel and leave in a warm place to rise for about 2 hours until doubled in bulk.

4 Lightly grease a large baking sheet. Turn the dough on to a floured surface, knead for 2 minutes, then divide into eight pieces. Shape the pieces into balls and flatten them with the palm of your hand to make neat 10cm/4in rounds.

5 Place the rounds on the prepared baking sheets, cover loosely with a large plastic bag (ballooning it to trap the air inside), and leave to stand in a warm place until the baps are well risen. Preheat the oven to 220°C/425°F/Gas 7.

6 Brush the baps with water, sprinkle with the oats and bake for about 20–25 minutes or until they sound hollow when tapped underneath. Cool on a wire rack, then serve with the low-fat filling of your choice.

Cook's Tip

To make a large loaf, shape the dough into a round, flatten it slightly and bake for 30–40 minutes. Test by tapping the base of the loaf – if it sounds hollow, it is cooked.

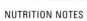

NUTRITION NOTES

Per portion

Energy	223Kcals/939kJ
Fat	1.14g
Saturated Fat	0.16g
Cholesterol	0
Fibre	3.1g

Rye Bread

Rye bread is popular in northern Europe and makes an excellent base for open sandwiches.

Makes 2 loaves

350g/12oz/3 cups strong wholemeal (whole-wheat) bread flour
225g/8oz/2 cups rye flour
115g/4oz/1 cup strong white bread flour
7.5ml/1½ tsp salt
30ml/2 tbsp caraway seeds
475ml/16fl oz/2 cups warm water
10ml/2 tsp dried yeast
pinch of sugar
30ml/2 tbsp molasses

Cook's Tip

To make caraway-seed bread rolls, divide each of the two flattened loaves into eight equal portions. Place them on the baking sheet brush with water and sprinkle with caraway seeds. Vary the topping by using poppy seeds if you prefer. Bake for 15–20 minutes.

NUTRITION NOTES

Per portion (serves 16)

Energy	156Kcals/655kJ
Fat	1.2g
Saturated Fat	0.05g
Cholesterol	0
Fibre	4.53g

1 Put the flours and salt in a bowl. Set aside 5ml/1 tsp of the caraway seeds and add the rest to the bowl.

2 Put half the water in a jug. Sprinkle the yeast on top. Add the sugar, mix well and leave for 10 minutes.

3 Make a well in the flour mixture, then add the yeast mixture with the molasses and the remaining water. Gradually incorporate the flour and mix to a soft dough, adding a little extra water if necessary.

4 Transfer to a floured surface and knead for 5 minutes until smooth and elastic. Return to the clean bowl, cover and leave in a warm place for about 2 hours until doubled in bulk. Grease a baking sheet.

5 Turn the dough on to a floured surface and knead for 2 minutes. Divide the dough in half, then shape into two 23cm/9in long oval loaves. Flatten the loaves slightly and place them on the baking sheet.

6 Brush the loaves with water and sprinkle with the remaining caraway seeds. Cover and leave in a warm place for about 40 minutes, until well risen. Preheat the oven to 200°C/400°F/Gas 6. Bake the loaves for about 30 minutes or until they sound hollow when tapped underneath. Cool on a wire rack. Serve the bread plain, or add a low-fat topping.

Cheese Bread

A tasty bread, perfect for making savoury sandwiches.

Makes 1 loaf
10ml/2 tsp dried yeast
250ml/8fl oz/1 cup lukewarm
skimmed milk
25g/1oz/2 tbsp butter
350g/12oz/3 cups strong white
bread flour
10ml/2 tsp salt
115g/4oz/1 cup grated mature (sharp)
Cheddar cheese

NUTRITION NOTES
Per portion (serves 10)

Energy	214Kcals/903kJ
Fat	4.8g
Saturated Fat	1.57g
Cholesterol	5.5mg
Fibre	1.4g

---

1 Combine the yeast and milk, stir, and leave for 15 minutes to dissolve. Melt the butter, let cool, and add to the yeast mixture.

2 Mix the flour and salt together in a large bowl. Make a well in the centre and pour in the yeast mixture. With a wooden spoon, stir from the centre, incorporating flour with each turn, to obtain a rough dough. If the dough seems too dry, add 30–45ml/ 2–3 tbsp water.

3 Transfer to a floured surface and knead until smooth and elastic. Return to the bowl, cover and leave to rise in a warm place until doubled in volume, for 2–3 hours.

4 Grease a 23 x 13 cm/9 x 5in bread tin (pan). Knock back (punch down) the dough with your fist. Knead in the cheese, distributing it as evenly as possible.

5 Twist the dough, form into a loaf shape and place in the tin, tucking the ends under. Leave to stand in a warm place until the dough rises above the rim of the tin.

6 Preheat the oven to 200°C/400°F/ Gas 6. Bake for 15 minutes, then lower the heat to 190°C/375°F/Gas 5 and bake for about 30 minutes more, until the bottom sounds hollow when tapped. Allow to cool on a rack.

Anadama Bread

A delicious traditional American yeast bread flavoured with molasses.

1 Combine the yeast and lukewarm water, stir well, and leave for 15 minutes to dissolve.

2 Meanwhile, combine the corn meal, butter or margarine, molasses and boiling water in a large bowl. Add the yeast, egg, and half of the flour. Stir together to blend.

3 Stir in the remaining flour and salt. When the dough becomes too stiff, stir with your hands until it comes away from the sides of the bowl. If it is too sticky, add more flour; if too stiff, add a little water.

4 Knead until smooth and elastic. Place in a bowl, cover with a plastic bag, and leave in a warm place until doubled in volume, for 2–3 hours.

5 Grease two 18 x 7.5cm/7in x 3in bread tins (pans). Knock back (punch down) the dough with your fist. Shape into two loaves and place in the tins, seam-side down. Cover and leave in a warm place until risen above the top of the tins, for 1–2 hours.

6 Preheat the oven to 190°C/375°F/Gas 5. Bake for 50 minutes. Remove and cool on a rack, or set across the tin to cool.

Makes 2 loaves

10ml/2 tsp dried yeast
60ml/4 tbsp lukewarm water
50g/2oz/½ cup corn meal
40g/1½oz/3 tbsp butter or margarine
60ml/4 tbsp molasses
175ml/6fl oz/¾ cup boiling water
1 egg
350g/12oz/3 cups strong white bread flour
10ml/2 tsp salt

NUTRITION NOTES

Per portion (serves 12)

Energy	146Kcals/616kJ
Fat	3.1g
Saturated Fat	1.62g
Cholesterol	18.5mg
Fibre	0.9g

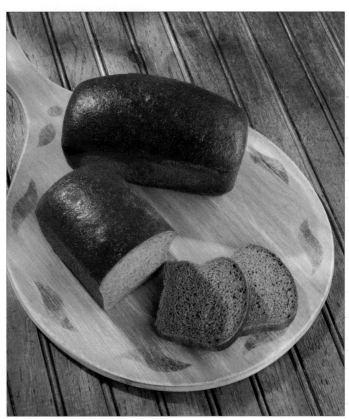

Rosemary and Sea Salt Focaccia

Focaccia is an Italian flat bread made with olive oil. Here it is given added flavour with rosemary and coarse sea salt.

Makes 1

350g/12oz/3 cups strong white bread flour
2.5ml/½ tsp salt
10ml/2 tsp easy-blend (rapid-rise) dried yeast
250ml/8fl oz/1 cup lukewarm water
45ml/3 tbsp olive oil
1 small red onion
leaves from 1 large rosemary sprig
5ml/1 tsp coarse sea salt

NUTRITION NOTES

Per portion (serves 8)

Energy	191Kcals/807kJ
Fat	4.72g
Saturated Fat	0.68g
Cholesterol	0
Fibre	1.46g

1 Sift the flour and salt into a large mixing bowl. Stir in the yeast, then make a well in the middle of the dry ingredients. Pour in the water and 30ml/2 tbsp of the oil. Mix well, adding a little more water if the mixture seems too dry.

2 Transfer the dough to a lightly floured surface and knead for about 10 minutes until smooth and elastic.

3 Place the dough in a greased bowl, cover and leave in a warm place for about 1 hour until doubled in size. Knock back (punch down) and knead the dough for 2–3 minutes.

4 Meanwhile, preheat the oven to 220°C/425°F/Gas 7. Roll out the dough to a large circle about 1cm/½in thick, and transfer to a greased baking sheet. Brush with the remaining oil.

5 Halve the onion and slice it into thin wedges. Sprinkle over the dough with the rosemary and sea salt, pressing lightly.

6 Make deep indentations in the dough with your finger. Cover the surface with greased clear film (plastic wrap) and leave the dough to rise in a warm place for 30 minutes. Remove the clear film and bake for 25–30 minutes until golden.

Onion Focaccia

This pizza-like flat bread is characterized by its soft dimpled surface.

Makes 2
675/1½lb/6 cups strong white
bread flour
2.5ml/½ tsp salt
2.5ml/½ tsp caster (superfine) sugar
15ml/1 tbsp easy-blend (rapid-rise)
dried yeast
60ml/4 tbsp extra virgin olive oil
450ml/¾ pint/scant 2 cups
hand-hot water

To finish
2 red onions, thinly sliced
45ml/3 tbsp extra virgin olive oil
15ml/1 tbsp coarse salt

1 Sift the flour, salt and sugar into a large bowl. Stir in the yeast, oil and water and mix to a dough using a round-bladed knife. (Add a little extra water if the dough is dry.)

2 Turn out on to a lightly floured surface and knead for about 10 minutes until smooth and elastic. Put the dough in a clean, lightly oiled bowl and cover with clear film (plastic wrap). Leave to rise in a warm place until doubled in bulk.

3 Place two 25cm/10in plain metal flan rings on baking sheets. Oil the sides of the rings and the baking sheets.

4 Preheat the oven to 200°C/400°F/ Gas 6. Halve the dough and roll each piece to a 25cm/10in round. Press into the tins, cover with a damp dishtowel and leave for 30 minutes to rise.

5 Make deep holes, about 2.5cm/1in apart, in the dough. Cover and leave for a further 20 minutes.

6 Scatter with the onions and drizzle over the oil. Sprinkle with the salt, then a little cold water, to stop a crust from forming.

7 Bake for about 25 minutes, sprinkling with water again during cooking. Cool on a wire rack.

NUTRITION NOTES
Per portion (serves 16)

Energy	202Kcals/847kJ
Fat	3.28g
Saturated Fat	0.46g
Cholesterol	0
Fibre	22.13g

Sun-dried Tomato Braid

This is a marvellous Mediterranean-flavoured bread to serve at a summer buffet or barbecue.

Makes 1 loaf

300ml/½ pint/1¼ cups warm water
5ml/1 tsp dried yeast
pinch of sugar
225g/8oz/2 cups strong wholemeal
(whole-wheat) bread flour
225g/8oz/2 cups strong white
bread flour
5ml/1 tsp salt
1.5ml/¼ tsp freshly ground
black pepper
50g/2oz/⅔ cup drained, chopped
sun-dried tomatoes in oil, plus
15ml/1 tbsp oil from the jar
25g/1oz/⅓ cup freshly grated
Parmesan cheese
30ml/2 tbsp red pesto
5ml/1 tsp coarse salt

Cook's Tip

If you are unable to locate red pesto, use 30ml/2 tbsp chopped fresh basil mixed with 15ml/1 tbsp sun-dried tomato purée (paste).

NUTRITION NOTES

Per portion (serves 8–10)

Energy	294Kcals/1233kJ
Fat	12.12g
Saturated Fat	2.13g
Cholesterol	3.4mg
Fibre	3.39g

1 Put half the warm water in a jug. Sprinkle the yeast on top. Add the sugar, mix well and leave for 10 minutes.

2 Put the wholemeal flour in a mixing bowl. Sift in the white flour, salt and pepper. Make a well in the centre and add the yeast mixture, sun-dried tomatoes, oil, Parmesan, pesto and the remaining water. Gradually incorporate the flour and mix to a soft dough, adding a little extra water if necessary.

3 Transfer the dough to a floured surface and knead for 5 minutes until smooth and elastic. Return to the clean bowl, cover with a damp dishtowel and leave in a warm place to rise for about 2 hours until doubled in bulk. Lightly grease a baking sheet.

4 Transfer the dough on to a lightly floured surface and knead for a few minutes. Divide the dough into three equal pieces and shape each into a 30cm/12in long sausage.

5 Dampen the ends of the three sausages. Press them together at one end, braid them loosely, then press them together at the other end. Place on the baking sheet, cover and leave in a warm place for 30 minutes until well risen. Preheat the oven to 220°C/425°F/Gas 7.

6 Sprinkle the braid with the coarse salt. Bake for 10 minutes, then lower the temperature to 200°C/400°F/Gas 6 and bake for a further 15–20 minutes, or until the loaf sounds hollow when tapped underneath. Cool on a wire rack.

Saffron Focaccia

A dazzling yellow bread with a distinctive flavour.

Makes 1
pinch of saffron threads
150ml/¼ pint/⅔ cup boiling water
225g/8oz/2 cups strong white
bread flour
2.5ml/½ tsp salt
5ml/1 tsp easy-blend (rapid-rise)
dried yeast
15ml/1 tbsp olive oil

For the topping
2 garlic cloves, sliced
1 red onion, cut into thin wedges
rosemary sprigs
12 black pitted olives,
coarsely chopped
15ml/1 tbsp olive oil

1 Infuse the saffron in the boiling water. Leave until cooled to lukewarm.

2 Place the flour, salt, yeast and olive oil in a food processor. Turn on and gradually add the saffron and its liquid until the dough forms a ball.

3 Transfer to a floured board and knead for 10–15 minutes. Place in a bowl, cover and leave to rise for about 30–40 minutes, until doubled in size.

4 Knock back (punch down) the risen dough on a lightly floured surface and roll out into an oval shape, 1cm/½in thick. Place on a lightly greased baking sheet and leave to rise for 20–30 minutes.

5 Preheat the oven to 200°C/400°F/Gas 6. Use your fingers to press small indentations in the dough.

6 Cover with the topping ingredients, brush lightly with olive oil, and bake for about 25 minutes or until the loaf sounds hollow when tapped on the bottom. Leave to cool.

NUTRITION NOTES

Per portion (serves 10)

Energy	104Kcals/439kJ
Fat	15.91g
Saturated Fat	4g
Cholesterol	0
Fibre	9.4g

Spinach and Bacon Bread

Use smoked lean back bacon for the best possible flavour with the minimum of fat for this tasty bread. One loaf will give you eight portions, so it is a good idea to freeze one of the loaves.

Makes 2 loaves

450ml/¾ pint/scant 2 cups warm water
10ml/2 tsp dried yeast
pinch of sugar
15ml/1 tbsp olive oil
1 onion, chopped
115g/4oz smoked bacon rashers (strips), chopped
225g/8oz chopped spinach, thawed if frozen
675g/1½lb/6 cups strong white bread flour
7.5ml/1½ tsp salt
7.5ml/1½ tsp freshly grated nutmeg
25g/1oz/¼ cup grated reduced-fat Cheddar cheese

Cook's Tip

If using frozen spinach, be sure to squeeze out any excess liquid or the resulting dough will be too sticky.

NUTRITION NOTES

Per portion (serves 16)

Energy	344Kcals/1446kJ
Fat	4.34g
Saturated Fat	0.72g
Cholesterol	3.94mg
Fibre	3.36g

1 Put the water in a bowl. Sprinkle the yeast on top and add the sugar. Mix well and leave for 10 minutes. Lightly grease two 23cm/9in cake tins (pans).

2 Heat the oil in a frying pan and fry the onion and bacon for 10 minutes until golden brown. Meanwhile, if using frozen spinach, drain it thoroughly.

3 Sift the flour, salt and nutmeg into a mixing bowl and make a well in the centre. Add the yeast mixture. Tip in the fried bacon and onion (with the oil), then add the spinach. Gradually incorporate the flour mixture and mix to a soft dough.

4 Transfer the dough to a floured surface and knead for 5 minutes until smooth and elastic. Return to the clean bowl, cover with a damp dishtowel and leave in a warm place to rise for about 2 hours, until doubled in bulk.

5 Transfer the dough to a floured surface, knead briefly, then divide it in half. Shape each half into a ball, flatten slightly and place in a tin, pressing the dough so that it extends to the edges. Mark each loaf into eight wedges and sprinkle with the cheese. Cover loosely with a plastic bag and leave in a warm place until well risen. Preheat the oven to 200°C/400°F/Gas 6.

6 Bake the loaves for 25–30 minutes, or until they sound hollow when they are tapped underneath. Transfer to a wire rack to cool.

Prosciutto and Parmesan Bread

This nourishing bread is almost a meal in itself.

Makes 1 loaf
225g/8oz/2 cups self-raising (self-rising) wholemeal (whole-wheat) flour
225g/8oz/2 cups self-raising (self-rising) white flour
5ml/1 tsp baking powder
5ml/1 tsp salt
5ml/1 tsp black pepper
75g/3oz prosciutto
25g/1oz/⅓ cup freshly grated Parmesan cheese
30ml/2 tbsp chopped fresh parsley
45ml/3 tbsp Meaux mustard
350ml/12fl oz/1½ cups buttermilk
skimmed milk, to glaze

NUTRITION NOTES
Per portion (serves 8)

Energy	250Kcals/1053kJ
Fat	3.65g
Saturated Fat	1.3g
Cholesterol	7.09mg
Fibre	3.81g

1 Preheat the oven to 200°C/400°F/ Gas 6. Flour a baking sheet. Place the wholemeal flour in a bowl and sift in the white flour, baking powder and salt. Add the pepper and the prosciutto. Set aside about 15ml/1 tbsp of the grated Parmesan and stir the rest into the flour mixture with the parsley. Make a well in the centre.

2 Mix the mustard and buttermilk together, pour into the flour and quickly mix to a soft dough.

3 Transfer the dough to a floured surface and knead briefly. Shape into an oval loaf, brush with milk and sprinkle with the reserved Parmesan cheese. Put the loaf on the prepared baking sheet.

4 Bake the loaf for 25–30 minutes, or until it sounds hollow when tapped underneath. Allow to cool before serving.

Caraway Breadsticks

Ideal to nibble with drinks, these can be made with all kinds of other seeds –
try cumin seeds, poppy seeds or celery seeds.

1 Grease two baking sheets. Put the warm water in a jug. Sprinkle the yeast on top. Add the sugar, mix well and leave for 10 minutes.

2 Sift the flour and salt into a mixing bowl, stir in the caraway seeds and make a well in the centre. Add the yeast mixture and gradually incorporate the flour to make a soft dough, adding a little water if necessary.

3 Preheat the oven to 220°C/425°F/ Gas 7. Transfer the dough to a lightly floured surface and knead for 5 minutes until smooth. Divide the mixture into 20 pieces and roll each piece into a 30cm/12in stick.

4 Arrange the sticks on the baking sheets, leaving room between them to allow for rising.

5 Bake the breadsticks for about 10–12 minutes until golden brown. Cool on the baking sheets.

Makes about 20

150ml/¼ pint/⅔ cup warm water
2.5ml/½ tsp dried yeast
pinch of sugar
225g/8oz/2 cups strong white
bread flour
2.5ml/½ tsp salt
10ml/2 tsp caraway seeds

NUTRITION NOTES
Per portion

Energy	45Kcals/189kJ
Fat	0.24g
Saturated Fat	0.02g
Cholesterol	0
Fibre	0.3g

Cheese and Onion Sticks

An extremely tasty bread which is very good with soups or salads. Use an extra-strong cheese to give plenty of flavour without piling on the fat.

Makes 2 loaves
300ml/½ pint/1¼ cups warm water
5ml/1 tsp dried yeast
pinch of sugar
15ml/1 tbsp sunflower oil
1 red onion, finely chopped
450g/1lb/4 cups strong white
bread flour
5ml/1 tsp salt
5ml/1 tsp dry mustard
45ml/3 tbsp chopped fresh herbs, such
as thyme, parsley, marjoram or sage
75g/3oz/¾ cup grated reduced-fat
Cheddar cheese

Variation
To make Onion and Coriander
Sticks, omit the cheese, herbs and
mustard. Add 15ml/1 tbsp ground
coriander and 45ml/3 tbsp
chopped fresh coriander
(cilantro) instead.

NUTRITION NOTES
Per portion (serves 8–12)

Energy	210Kcals/882kJ
Fat	3.16g
Saturated Fat	0.25g
Cholesterol	3.22mg
Fibre	1.79g

1 Put the water in a jug. Sprinkle the yeast on top. Add the sugar, mix well and leave for 10 minutes.

2 Heat the oil in a small frying pan and fry the onion until it is well coloured.

3 Stir the flour, salt and mustard into a mixing bowl, then add the chopped herbs. Set aside 30ml/2 tbsp of the cheese. Stir the rest into the flour mixture and make a well in the centre. Add the yeast mixture with the fried onions and oil, then gradually incorporate the flour and mix to a soft dough, adding extra water if necessary.

4 Transfer the dough to a floured surface and knead for 5 minutes until smooth and elastic. Return to the clean bowl, cover with a damp dishtowel and leave in a warm place to rise for about 2 hours, until doubled in bulk. Lightly grease two baking sheets.

5 Transfer the dough on to a floured surface, knead briefly, then divide the mixture in half and roll each piece into a 30cm/12in long stick. Place each stick on a baking sheet and make diagonal cuts along the top.

6 Sprinkle the sticks with the reserved cheese. Cover and leave for 30 minutes until well risen. Preheat the oven to 220°C/425°F/Gas 7. Bake the sticks for 25 minutes or until they sound hollow when tapped underneath.

Saffron and Basil Breadsticks

Saffron lends its delicate aroma and flavour, as well as rich yellow colour, to these tasty breadsticks.

Makes 32

generous pinch of saffron threads
30ml/2 tbsp hot water
450g/1lb/4 cups strong white
bread flour
5ml/1 tsp salt
10ml/2 tsp easy-blend (rapid-rise)
dried yeast
300ml/½ pint/1¼ cups lukewarm water
45ml/3 tbsp olive oil
45ml/3 tbsp chopped fresh basil

1 Infuse the saffron threads in the hot water for 10 minutes.

2 Sift the flour and salt into a large mixing bowl. Stir in the yeast, then make a well in the centre of the dry ingredients. Pour in the lukewarm water and saffron liquid and mix a little.

3 Add the oil and basil and continue to mix to a soft dough.

4 Turn out and knead the dough on a lightly floured surface for about 10 minutes until smooth and elastic. Place in a greased bowl, cover with clear film (plastic wrap) and leave for about 1 hour until it has doubled in size.

5 Knock back (punch down) and knead the dough on a lightly floured surface for 2–3 minutes.

6 Preheat the oven to 220°C/425°F/ Gas 7. Divide the dough into 32 pieces and shape into long sticks. Place well apart on greased baking sheets, then leave for a further 15– 20 minutes until they become puffy. Bake for about 15 minutes until crisp and golden. Serve warm.

NUTRITION NOTES

Per portion	
Energy	59Kcals/249kJ
Fat	1.3g
Saturated Fat	1.17g
Cholesterol	0
Fibre	0.4g

Cook's Tip

Use powdered saffron if saffron threads are not available. Turmeric is an inexpensive alternative: it imparts a lovely gold colour, but its flavour is not as delicate.

Olive and Herb Bread

Olive breads are popular all over the Mediterranean. For this Greek recipe use rich oily olives or those marinated in herbs, rather than canned ones.

Makes 2 loaves

2 red onions, thinly sliced
30ml/2 tbsp olive oil
225g/8oz/2 cups pitted black or
green olives
800g/1¾lb/7 cups strong white bread flour
7.5ml/1½ tsp salt
20ml/4 tsp easy-blend (rapid-rise)
dried yeast
45ml/3 tbsp roughly chopped parsley,
coriander (cilantro) or mint
457ml/16fl oz/2 cups hand-hot water

NUTRITION NOTES

Per portion (serves 20)

Energy	157Kcals/664kJ
Fat	2.9g
Saturated Fat	0.41g
Cholesterol	0
Fibre	1.8g

1 Fry the onions in the oil until soft. Roughly chop the olives.

2 Put the flour, salt, yeast and parsley, coriander or mint in a large bowl with the olives and fried onions and pour in the water. Mix to a dough using a round-bladed knife, adding a little more water if the mixture feels dry.

3 Transfer to a lightly floured surface and knead for about 10 minutes. Put in a clean bowl, cover with clear film (plastic wrap) and leave in a warm place until doubled in bulk.

4 Preheat the oven to 220°C/425°F/ Gas 7. Lightly grease two baking sheets. Turn the dough on to a floured surface and cut in half. Shape into two rounds and place on the baking sheets. Cover loosely with lightly oiled clear film and leave until doubled in size.

5 Slash the tops of the loaves with a knife, then bake for about 40 minutes or until the loaves sound hollow when tapped on the bottom. Transfer to a wire rack to cool.

Variation

Shape the dough into 16 small rolls. Slash the tops as above and reduce the cooking time to 25 minutes.

Tomato Breadsticks

Once you've tried this simple recipe, you'll never buy manufactured breadsticks again.
Serve as a snack, or with aperitifs and a dip at the beginning of a meal.

1 Place the flour, salt and yeast in a food processor. Add the honey and olive oil and, with the machine running, gradually pour in the water (you may not need it all as flours vary). Stop adding water as soon as the dough starts to cling together. Process for 1 minute more.

2 Transfer the dough to a floured surface and knead for 3–4 minutes until springy and smooth.

3 Knead in the chopped sun-dried tomatoes. Form into a ball and place in a lightly oiled bowl. Leave to rise for 5 minutes.

4 Preheat the oven to 150°C/300°F/ Gas 2. Divide the dough into 16 pieces and roll each piece into a 28 x 1cm/11 x ½in long stick. Place on a lightly oiled baking sheet and leave to rise in a warm place for 15 minutes.

Variation
Instead of sun-dried tomatoes, you could try making these breadsticks with reduced-fat Cheddar cheese, sesame seeds or herbs.

5 Brush the sticks with milk and sprinkle with poppy seeds. Bake for 30 minutes. Leave to cool on a wire cooling rack.

Makes 16
225g/8oz/2 cups strong white bread flour
2.5ml/½ tsp salt
2.5ml/½ tsp easy-blend (rapid-rise) dried yeast
5ml/1 tsp honey
5ml/1 tsp olive oil
about 150ml/¼ pint/⅔ cup warm water
6 halves sun-dried tomatoes in olive oil, drained and chopped
15ml/1 tbsp skimmed milk
10ml/2 tsp poppy seeds

NUTRITION NOTES
Per portion

Energy	82Kcals/346kJ
Fat	3.53g
Saturated Fat	0.44g
Cholesterol	0
Fibre	0.44g

Sourdough Bread

Sourdough bread has a slightly sour, tangy flavour created by using a special yeast starter as the leavener.

Makes 1 loaf
350g/12oz/3 cups plain
(all-purpose) flour
15ml/1 tbsp salt
120ml/4fl oz/½ cup lukewarm water

For the starter

175ml/6fl oz/¾ cup lukewarm water
50g/2oz/½ cup plain (all-purpose) flour

Cook's Tip
The starter can be chilled for up to one week, but must be brought back to room temperature before using.

NUTRITION NOTES
Per portion (serves 10)

Energy	179Kcals/763kJ
Fat	0.7g
Saturated Fat	0.1g
Cholesterol	0
Fibre	1.6g

1 For the starter, combine the yeast and water, stir and leave for 15 minutes to dissolve.

2 Sprinkle over the flour and whisk until it forms a batter; it does not have to be smooth. Cover and leave to rise in a warm place for at least 24 hours, or preferably 2–4 days, before using.

3 For the bread, combine the flour and salt in a large bowl. Make a well in the centre and add the starter and water. With a wooden spoon, stir from the centre, incorporating more flour with each turn, to obtain a rough dough.

4 Transfer the dough to a floured surface. To knead, push the dough away from you with the palm of your hand, then fold it towards you, and push it away again. Repeat the process until the dough has become smooth and elastic.

5 Place in a clean bowl, cover, and leave to rise in a warm place until doubled in volume, for about 2 hours. Lightly grease a 20 x 10cm/8 x 4in loaf tin (pan).

6 Knock back (punch down) the dough with your fist. Knead briefly, then form into a loaf shape and place in the tin, seam-side down. Cover with a plastic bag, and leave to rise in a warm place until the dough rises above the rim of the tin, for about 1½ hours.

7 Preheat the oven to 220°C/425°F/ Gas 7. Dust the top of the loaf with flour, then score lengthways. Bake for 15 minutes. Lower the heat to 190°C/ 375°F/Gas 5 and bake for 30 minutes more, or until the bottom sounds hollow when tapped.

Potato Bread

A recipe for a traditional loaf – that is low in fat.

Makes 2 loaves
60ml/4 tsp dried yeast
250ml/8fl oz/1 cup lukewarm
skimmed milk
675g/½lb potatoes, boiled (reserve
250ml/8fl oz/1 cup of potato
cooking liquid)
30ml/2 tbsp oil
20ml/4 tsp salt
675–800g/1½–1¾lb/6–7 cups strong
white bread flour

NUTRITION NOTES
Per portion (serves 16)

Energy	177Kcals/751kJ
Fat	1.7g
Saturated Fat	0.2g
Cholesterol	0
Fibre	1.5g

1 Combine the yeast and the milk in a large bowl and leave to dissolve for about 15 minutes. Mash the potatoes.

2 Add the potatoes, oil and salt to the yeast mixture and mix well. Stir in 250ml/8fl oz/1 cup of the cooking water, then stir in the flour, 115g/4oz/1 cup at a time, to form a stiff dough.

3 Transfer to a floured surface and knead until smooth and elastic. Return to the bowl, cover and leave in a warm place until doubled in size, for 1–1½ hours. Knock back (punch down), then leave to rise for another 40 minutes.

4 Grease two 23 x 13cm/9 x 5in loaf tins (pans). Roll the dough into 20 small balls. Place two rows of balls in each tin. Leave until the dough has risen above the rim of the tins.

5 Preheat the oven to 200°C/400°F/ Gas 6. Bake for 10 minutes, then lower the heat to 190°C/375°F/Gas 5 and bake for about 40 minutes, or until the bottoms sound hollow when tapped. Cool on a rack.

Irish Soda Bread

This is a solid bread – delicious with salad and pickles.

1 Preheat the oven to 200°C/400°F/ Gas 6. Grease a baking sheet.

2 Sift the flours, bicarbonate of soda and salt together in a bowl. Make a well in the centre and add the butter or margarine and buttermilk. Working outward from the centre, stir with a fork until a soft dough is formed.

6 Dust with flour. Bake until brown, for 40–50 minutes. Transfer to a wire rack to cool.

Makes 1 loaf

225g/8oz/2 cups plain (all-purpose) flour
225g/8oz/1 cup plain (all-purpose) wholemeal (whole-wheat) flour
5ml/1 tsp bicarbonate of soda (baking soda)
5ml/1 tsp salt
30ml/2 tbsp butter or margarine
350ml/12fl oz/1½ cups buttermilk
15ml/1 tbsp flour, for dusting

NUTRITION NOTES

Per portion (serves 10)

Energy	188Kcals/797kJ
Fat	3.3g
Saturated Fat	0.7g
Cholesterol	1mg
Fibre	2.3g

3 With floured hands, gather the dough into a ball.

4 Transfer to a floured surface and knead for 3 minutes. Shape the dough into a large round.

5 Place on the baking sheet. Cut a cross in the top with a sharp knife.

Brown Soda Bread

This is very easy to make – simply mix and bake. Instead of yeast, bicarbonate of soda and cream of tartar are the raising agents. This is an excellent recipe for those new to breadmaking.

Makes 1 loaf

450g/1lb/4 cups plain (all-purpose) flour
450g/1lb/4 cups plain (all-purpose) wholemeal (whole-wheat) flour
10ml/2 tsp salt
15ml/1 tbsp bicarbonate of soda (baking soda)
20ml/4 tsp cream of tartar
10ml/2 tsp caster (superfine) sugar
50g/2oz/¼ cup butter
about 900ml/1½ pints/3¾ cups buttermilk or skimmed milk

NUTRITION NOTES

Per portion (serves 20)

Energy	185Kcals/784kJ
Fat	2.9g
Saturated Fat	0.53g
Cholesterol	1.1mg
Fibre	2.8g

1 Lightly grease a baking sheet. Preheat the oven to 190°C/375°F/Gas 5.

2 Sift all the dry ingredients into a large bowl, tipping any bran from the flour back into the bowl.

3 Rub the butter into the flour mixture, then add enough buttermilk or milk to make a soft dough. You may not need all of it, so add it cautiously.

4 Knead the dough lightly until smooth – do not overknead – then transfer to the baking sheet and shape to a large round about 5cm/2in thick.

5 Using the floured handle of a wooden spoon, make a large cross on top of the dough. Sprinkle over a little extra wholemeal flour.

6 Bake for 40–50 minutes until risen and firm. Cool for 5 minutes before transferring to a wire rack to cool further.

Sage Soda Bread

This wonderful loaf, quite unlike bread made with yeast, has a velvety texture and a powerful aroma of sage.

1 Preheat the oven to 220°C/425°F/ Gas 7. Sift the dry ingredients into a mixing bowl.

4 Cut a deep cross in the top. Bake in the oven for about 40 minutes until the loaf is well risen and sounds hollow when tapped on the bottom. Leave to cool on a wire rack.

2 Stir in the sage and add enough buttermilk to make a soft dough.

3 Shape the dough into a round loaf with your hands and place on a lightly oiled baking sheet.

Makes 1 loaf
175g/6oz/1½ cups plain (all-purpose) wholemeal (whole-wheat) flour
115g/4oz/1 cup strong white bread flour
2.5ml/½ tsp salt
5ml/1 tsp bicarbonate of soda (baking soda)
30ml/2 tbsp shredded fresh sage or
10ml/2 tsp dried sage
300–450ml/½–¾ pint/
1¼–scant 2 cups buttermilk

NUTRITION NOTES
Per portion (serves 10)
Energy	125Kcals/525kJ
Fat	9.2g
Saturated Fat	0.2g
Cholesterol	0.7mg
Fibre	2.81g

Variation
As an alternative to the sage, try using either finely chopped rosemary or thyme.

Spiral Herb Bread

An attractive and delicious bread that is ideal for serving with a salad for a healthy lunch.

Makes 2 loaves
425g/15oz/3⅔ cups strong white
bread flour
15ml/1 tbsp salt
30ml/2 tbsp easy-blend (rapid-rise)
dried yeast
550ml/18fl oz/2½ cups lukewarm water
25g/1oz/2 tbsp sunflower margarine
large bunch of parsley, finely chopped
bunch of spring onions (scallions), chopped
garlic clove, finely chopped
salt and ground black pepper
1 egg, lightly beaten

NUTRITION NOTES

Per portion (serves 20)	
Energy	85Kcals/356kJ
Fat	1.22g
Saturated Fat	0.49g
Cholesterol	7.24mg
Fibre	1.54g

1 Combine the flour, salt and yeast in a large bowl. Make a well in the centre and pour in the water. With a wooden spoon, stir from the centre, working outwards to obtain a rough dough.

2 Transfer the dough to a floured surface and knead until smooth and elastic. Return to the bowl, cover with a plastic bag, and leave for about 2 hours until doubled in volume.

3 Meanwhile, combine the margarine, parsley, spring onions and garlic in a large frying pan. Cook over a low heat, stirring until softened. Season with salt and pepper and set aside.

4 Grease two 23 x 13cm/9 x 5in loaf tins (pans). When the dough has risen, cut in half and roll each half into a rectangle about 35 x 23cm/14 x 9in. Brush both with the beaten egg. Divide the herb mixture between the two, spreading just up to the edges.

5 Roll up to enclose the filling and pinch the short ends to seal. Place in the tins, seam-side down. Cover the dough with a clean dishtowel and leave undisturbed in a warm place until the dough rises above the rim of the tins.

6 Preheat the oven to 190°C/375°F/ Gas 5. Brush the loaves with milk and bake for about 55 minutes, until the bottoms sound hollow when tapped. Cool on a wire rack.

Walnut Bread

Delicious at any time of day, this bread may be eaten plain or topped with low-fat cream cheese.

1 Mix together the flours and salt in a large bowl. Make a well in the centre and pour in 250ml/8fl oz/1 cup of the water, the honey and the yeast. Set aside until the yeast dissolves and the mixture is frothy.

2 Add the remaining water. With a wooden spoon, stir from the centre, incorporating flour with each turn, to obtain a smooth dough. Add more flour to the bowl if the dough is too sticky and use your hands if the dough becomes too stiff to stir.

3 Transfer to a floured board and knead, adding flour if necessary, until the dough is smooth and elastic. Place in a greased bowl and roll the dough around in the bowl to coat thoroughly all over.

6 Preheat the oven to 220°C/425°F/ Gas 7. With a sharp knife, score the top of the loaf and brush with an egg glaze, if you like. Bake for 15 minutes. Lower the temperature to 190°C/375°F/ Gas 5 and bake for about 40 minutes, or until the bottom of the loaf sounds hollow when tapped. Leave to cool.

Makes 1 loaf
425g/15oz/3⅔ cups strong wholemeal (whole-wheat) bread flour
150g/5oz/1¼ cups strong white bread flour
12.5ml/2½ tsp salt
525ml/17fl oz/2¼ cups lukewarm water
15ml/1 tbsp clear honey
15ml/1 tbsp easy-blend (rapid-rise) dried yeast
150g/5oz/1¼ cups walnut pieces, plus extra for decorating

NUTRITION NOTES
Per portion (serves 10)

Energy	285Kcals/1198kJ
Fat	10.93g
Saturated Fat	1.2g
Cholesterol	7.7mg
Fibre	4.7g

4 Cover with a plastic bag and leave in a warm place until doubled in volume, about 1½ hours.

5 Knock back (punch down) the dough very firmly and knead in the walnuts. Shape the dough into a round loaf and place on a greased baking sheet. Press in the walnut pieces to decorate the top. Cover loosely with a damp dishtowel and leave in a warm place for about 25–30 minutes until doubled in size.

Oatmeal Bread

A healthy bread with a delightfully crumbly texture due to the inclusion of rolled oats.

Makes 2 loaves

475ml/16fl oz/2 cups skimmed milk
25g/1oz/2 tbsp low-fat margarine
50g/2oz/¼ cup soft dark brown sugar
10ml/2 tsp salt
15ml/1 tbsp easy-blend (rapid-rise)
dried yeast
50ml/2fl oz/¼ cup lukewarm water
400g/14oz/4 cups rolled oats
450–675g/1–1½lb/4–6 cups strong
white bread flour

NUTRITION NOTES

Per portion (serves 20)

Energy	228Kcals/958kJ
Fat	3.44g
Saturated Fat	1.19g
Cholesterol	3.9mg
Fibre	2.41g

1 Scald the milk. Remove from the heat and stir in the margarine, sugar and salt. Leave until lukewarm.

2 Combine the yeast and lukewarm water in a large bowl and leave until the yeast is dissolved and the mixture is frothy. Stir in the milk mixture.

3 Add 275g/10oz/3 cups of the oats and enough flour to obtain a soft pliable dough.

4 Transfer to a floured surface and knead until smooth and elastic.

5 Place the dough in a greased bowl, cover with a plastic bag, and leave for about 2–3 hours, until doubled in volume. Grease a large baking sheet.

6 Transfer the dough to a lightly floured surface and divide in half.

7 Shape into rounds. Place on the baking sheet, cover with a damp dishtowel and leave to rise for about 1 hour, until doubled in volume.

8 Preheat the oven to 200°C/400°F/ Gas 6. Score the tops of the loaves and sprinkle with the remaining oats. Bake for about 45–50 minutes, until the bottoms sound hollow when tapped. Cool on wire racks.

Squash and Nut Loaf

A moist and crunchy loaf, made with courgette and walnuts, this is a real treat.

1 Preheat the oven to 180°C/350°F/ Gas 4. Grease the base and sides of a 900g/2lb loaf tin (pan) and line with baking parchment.

2 Beat the eggs and sugar together and gradually add the oil.

3 Sift the flour into a bowl together with the baking powder, bicarbonate of soda, cinnamon and allspice.

4 Mix in the egg mixture with the rest of the ingredients, reserving 15ml/1 tbsp of the sunflower seeds for the top.

5 Spoon into the loaf tin, level off the top, and sprinkle with the reserved sunflower seeds.

6 Bake for about 1 hour or until a skewer inserted in the centre comes out clean. Leave to cool slightly, then turn out on to a wire cooling rack.

Makes 1 loaf

3 eggs
75g/3oz/⅓ cup soft light brown sugar
50ml/2fl oz/¼ cup sunflower oil
225g/8oz/2 cups plain (all-purpose) wholemeal (whole-wheat) flour
5ml/1 tsp baking powder
5ml/1 tsp bicarbonate of soda (baking soda)
5ml/1 tsp ground cinnamon
2.5ml/½ tsp ground allspice
7.5ml/1½ tsp green cardamoms, seeds removed and crushed
150g/5oz/1 cup coarsely grated courgette (zucchini)
50g/2oz/½ cup walnuts, chopped
50g/2oz/⅓ cup sunflower seeds

NUTRITION NOTES

Per portion (serves 10)

Energy	307Kcals/1290kJ
Fat	20.19g
Saturated Fat	2.64g
Cholesterol	65.45mg
Fibre	2.86g

Italian Flat Bread with Sage

This bread is perfect served hot to accompany a pasta supper.

Makes 1 loaf
10ml/2 tsp dried yeast
250ml/8fl oz/1 cup lukewarm water
375g/13oz/generous 3 cups strong
white bread flour
10ml/2 tsp salt
75ml/5 tbsp extra virgin olive oil
12 fresh sage leaves, chopped

NUTRITION NOTES

Per portion (serves 10)

Energy	205Kcals/864kJ
Fat	6.1g
Saturated Fat	0.6g
Cholesterol	0
Fibre	1.4g

1 Combine the yeast and water, stir and leave for 15 minutes to dissolve.

2 Mix the flour and salt in a large bowl and make a well in the centre.

3 Stir in the yeast mixture and 60ml/4 tbsp of the oil. Stir from the centre, incorporating flour with each turn, to obtain a rough dough.

4 Transfer to a floured surface and knead until smooth and elastic. Place in a lightly oiled bowl. Cover and leave to rise in a warm place until doubled in volume, for about 2 hours.

5 Preheat the oven to 200°C/400°F/ Gas 6 and place a baking sheet in the centre of the oven.

6 Knock back (punch down) the dough. Knead in the sage leaves, then roll into a 30cm/12in round. Leave to rise slightly.

7 Dimple the surface all over with your finger. Drizzle the remaining oil on top. Slide a floured board under the bread, carry to the oven, and slide off on to the hot baking sheet. Bake for about 35 minutes, or until golden brown. Cool on a rack.

Squash Yeast Bread

The grated courgettes give extra moisture to this tasty loaf.

1 In a colander, alternate layers of grated courgettes and salt. Leave for 30 minutes, then squeeze out the moisture with your hands.

2 Combine the yeast with 50ml/2fl oz/ ¼ cup of the lukewarm water, stir and leave for 15 minutes to dissolve the yeast.

3 Place the courgettes, yeast and flour in a bowl. Stir together and add just enough of the remaining water to obtain a rough dough.

4 Transfer to a floured surface and knead until smooth and elastic. Return the dough to the bowl, cover with a plastic bag, and leave to rise in a warm place until doubled in volume, for about 1½ hours.

5 Grease a baking sheet. Knock back (punch down) the risen dough with your fist and knead into a tapered cylinder. Place on the baking sheet, cover and leave to rise in a warm place until doubled in volume, for about 45 minutes.

6 Preheat the oven to 220°C/425°F/ Gas 7. Brush the bread with olive oil and bake for about 40–45 minutes, or until the loaf is a golden colour. Cool on a rack before serving.

Makes 1 loaf

450g/1lb/3½ cups courgettes (zucchini), grated
30ml/2 tbsp salt
10ml/2tsp dried yeast
300ml/½ pint/1¼ cups lukewarm water
400g/14oz/3½ cups strong white bread flour
olive oil, for brushing

NUTRITION NOTES

Per portion (serves 10)

Energy	191Kcals/811kJ
Fat	1.2g
Saturated Fat	0.2g
Cholesterol	0
Fibre	2g

Rosemary Bread

Sliced thinly, this herb bread is delicious with soup for a light meal.

Makes 1 loaf

7g/¼ oz easy-blend (rapid-rise)
dried yeast
175g/6oz/1½ cups strong wholemeal
(whole-wheat) bread flour
175g/6oz/1½ cups self-raising
(self-rising) white flour
10ml/2 tsp butter, melted, plus
extra for greasing
50ml/2fl oz/¼ cup warm water
250ml/8fl oz/1 cup skimmed milk
15ml/1 tbsp caster (superfine) sugar
5ml/1 tsp salt
15ml/1 tbsp sesame seeds
15ml/1 tbsp dried chopped onion
15ml/1 tbsp fresh rosemary leaves,
plus extra to decorate
115g/4oz/1 cup cubed Cheddar cheese
coarse salt

NUTRITION NOTES

Per portion (serves 10)

Energy	188Kcals/795kJ
Fat	5.6g
Saturated Fat	1.7g
Cholesterol	6mg
Fibre	2.2g

1 Mix the easy-blend dried yeast with the flours in a large mixing bowl. Add the melted butter. Stir in the warm water, milk, sugar, salt, sesame seeds, onion and rosemary. Knead thoroughly until quite smooth.

2 Flatten the dough, then add the cheese cubes. Quickly knead them in until they are well combined.

3 Place the dough in a large clean bowl greased with a little butter, turning it so that it becomes lightly greased on all sides. Cover with a clean, dry cloth. Put the greased bowl and dough in a warm place for about 1½ hours, or until the dough has risen and doubled in size.

4 Grease a 23 x 13cm/9 x 5in loaf tin (pan) with the remaining butter. Knock back (punch down) the dough to remove some of the air, and shape it into a loaf. Put the loaf into the tin, cover with the clean cloth used earlier and leave for about 1 hour until it has doubled in size once again. Preheat the oven to 190°C/375°F/Gas 5.

5 Bake for 30 minutes. During the last 5–10 minutes of baking, cover the loaf with foil to prevent it from becoming too dark. Remove from the loaf tin and leave to cool on a wire rack. Decorate with rosemary leaves and coarse salt scattered on top.

Dill Bread

Herb bread makes a tasty change at any mealtime.

1 Mix together the yeast, water and sugar in a large bowl and leave for 15 minutes to dissolve.

2 Stir in 350g/12oz/3 cups of the flour. Cover and leave to rise in a warm place for 45 minutes.

3 Cook the onion in 15ml/1 tbsp of the oil until soft. Set aside to cool, then stir into the yeast mixture. Stir in the dill, eggs, cottage cheese, salt and remaining oil into the yeast mixture. Gradually add the remaining flour until too stiff to stir.

4 Transfer to a floured surface and knead until smooth and elastic. Place in a bowl, cover, and leave to rise until doubled in volume, for 1–1½ hours.

5 Grease a large baking sheet. Cut the dough in half and shape into two rounds. Leave to rise in a warm place for 30 minutes.

6 Preheat the oven to 190°C/375°F/ Gas 5. Score the tops, brush with the milk, and bake until browned, about 50 minutes. Cool on a rack.

Makes 2 loaves
20ml/4 tsp dried yeast
475ml/16fl oz/2 cups lukewarm water
30ml/2 tbsp caster (superfine) sugar
850g/1lb 14oz/7½ cups strong white bread flour
½ onion, chopped
60ml/4 tbsp oil
1 large bunch of dill, finely chopped
2 eggs, lightly beaten
115g/4oz/½ cup cottage cheese
20ml/4 tsp salt
milk, for glazing

NUTRITION NOTES
Per portion (serves 20)

Energy	237Kcals/1003kJ
Fat	3.7g
Saturated Fat	0.6g
Cholesterol	20mg
Fibre	1.8g

Naan

There are various recipes for making naan, but this one is particularly easy to follow. Always serve naan warm, preferably straight from the grill, or wrap them in foil until you are ready to serve the meal.

Makes 6

5ml/1 tsp caster (superfine) sugar
5ml/1 tsp dried yeast
150ml/¼ pint/⅔ cup lukewarm water
225g/8oz/2 cups strong white bread flour
5ml/1 tsp ghee or butter
5ml/1 tsp salt
50g/2oz/¼ cup low-fat margarine, melted
5ml/1 tsp poppy seeds

NUTRITION NOTES

Per portion	
Energy	177Kcals/744kJ
Fat	5.07g
Saturated Fat	1.24g
Cholesterol	0.5mg
Fibre	0.2g

1 Put the sugar and yeast in a small bowl, add the warm water and mix well until the yeast has dissolved. Leave for 10 minutes or until the mixture becomes frothy.

2 Place the flour in a large mixing bowl, make a well in the middle and add the ghee or butter, and salt, then pour in the yeast mixture.

3 Mix well, using your hands, to make a dough, adding some more water if the dough is too dry. Turn out on to a floured surface and knead for about 5 minutes or until smooth.

4 Place the dough back in the clean bowl, cover with foil and leave to rise in a warm place for 1½ hours or until doubled in size.

5 Preheat the grill (broiler) to very hot. Transfer the dough to a floured surface and knead for a further 2 minutes. Break off small balls with your hand and roll into rounds about 12cm/4½in in diameter and 1cm/½in thick.

6 Place on a sheet of greased foil and grill (broil) for 7–10 minutes, turning twice to brush with margarine and sprinkle with poppy seeds.

Wholemeal Chapatis

These Indian breads are best served hot from the pan – but can be kept warm in foil.

1 Place the flour and salt in a mixing bowl. Make a well in the middle and gradually stir in the water, mixing well with your fingers.

2 Form a supple dough and knead for 7–10 minutes. Ideally, cover with clear film (plastic wrap) and leave on one side for 15–20 minutes. If time is short, roll out straight away.

3 Divide the dough into 8–10 equal portions. Roll out each piece to a round on a well-floured surface.

4 Place a heavy frying pan over a high heat. When steam rises from it, lower the heat to medium and add the first chapati to the pan.

5 When the chapati begins to bubble, turn it over. Press down with a clean dishtowel or a flat spoon and turn once again. Remove from the pan and keep warm in foil. Repeat the process until all the chapatis are cooked.

Makes 8–10

225g/8oz/2 cups plain (all-purpose) wholemeal (whole-wheat) flour
2.5ml/½ tsp salt
175ml/6fl oz/¾ cup water

NUTRITION NOTES

Per portion

Energy	87Kcals/366kJ
Fat	0.62g
Saturated Fat	0.08g
Cholesterol	0
Fibre	1.3g

Teabreads

These light and tasty
teabreads use the natural
sweetness of fruit and
honey for a mid-afternoon
energy-boosting treat that
won't weigh you down.

Banana and Cardamom Bread

The combination of banana and cardamom is delicious in this soft-textured moist loaf.
It is perfect for tea time, served with low-fat spread and jam.

Makes 1 loaf

150ml/¼ pint/⅔ cup lukewarm water
5ml/1 tsp dried yeast
pinch of sugar
10 cardamom pods
400g/14oz/3½ cups strong white
bread flour
5ml/1 tsp salt
30ml/2 tbsp malt extract
2 ripe bananas, mashed
5ml/1 tsp sesame seeds

1 Put the warm water in a small bowl. Sprinkle the yeast on top. Add the sugar, mix well and leave for 10 minutes.

2 Split the cardamom pods. Remove the seeds and chop them finely.

3 Sift the flour and salt into a mixing bowl and make a well in the centre. Add the yeast mixture with the malt extract, chopped cardamom seeds and bananas.

4 Gradually incorporate the flour and mix to a soft dough, adding a little extra water if necessary. Turn the dough on to a floured surface and knead for about 5 minutes until smooth and elastic. Return to the clean bowl, cover with a damp dishtowel and leave to rise for about 2 hours, until doubled in bulk.

5 Grease a baking sheet. Turn the dough on to a floured surface, knead briefly, then divide into three and shape into a braid. Place the braid on the baking sheet and cover loosely with a large plastic bag (ballooning it to trap the air). Leave until well risen. Preheat the oven to 220°C/425°F/Gas 7.

6 Brush the braid lightly with water and sprinkle with the sesame seeds. Bake for 10 minutes, then lower the oven temperature to 200°C/400°F/Gas 6. Cook for 15 minutes more, or until the loaf sounds hollow when it is tapped underneath. Cool on a wire rack.

Cook's Tip

Make sure that the bananas are really ripe, so that they impart maximum flavour to the bread. If you prefer, place the dough in one piece in a 450g/1lb loaf tin (pan) and bake for an extra 5 minutes. As well as being low in fat, bananas are a good source of potassium, therefore making an ideal nutritious, low-fat snack.

NUTRITION NOTES
Per portion (serves 6)

Energy	299Kcals/1254kJ
Fat	1.55g
Saturated Fat	0.23g
Cholesterol	0
Fibre	2.65g

Banana Orange Loaf

For the best banana flavour and a really good, moist texture, make sure the bananas are very ripe for this cake.

Makes 1 loaf

90g/3½oz/¾ cup plain (all-purpose) wholemeal (whole-wheat) flour
90g/3½oz/¾ cup plain (all-purpose) flour
5ml/1 tsp baking powder
5ml/1 tsp mixed (apple pie) spice
45ml/3 tbsp flaked (sliced) hazelnuts, toasted
2 large ripe bananas
1 egg
30ml/2 tbsp sunflower oil
30ml/2 tbsp clear honey
finely grated rind and juice of 1 small orange
4 orange slices, halved
10ml/2 tsp icing (confectioners') sugar

NUTRITION NOTES

Per portion (serves 8)

Energy	217Kcals/911kJ
Fat	7.59g
Saturated Fat	0.92g
Cholesterol	24.06mg
Fibre	2.46g

1 Preheat the oven to 180°C/350°F/ Gas 4.

2 Brush a 1 litre/1¾ pint/4 cup loaf tin (pan) with sunflower oil and line the base with baking parchment.

3 Sift the wholemeal flour and plain flour with the baking powder and spice into a large bowl, adding any bran caught in the sieve. Stir the toasted hazelnuts into the dry ingredients.

4 Peel and mash the bananas. Beat together with the egg, oil, honey and the orange rind and juice. Stir evenly into the dry ingredients.

5 Spoon the mixture into the prepared tin and smooth the top. Bake for 40–45 minutes, or until firm and golden brown. Turn out and cool on a wire rack. Sprinkle the orange slices with the icing sugar and grill (broil) until golden. Use to decorate the cake.

Cook's Tip

If you plan to keep the loaf for more than two or three days, omit the orange slices, brush with honey and sprinkle with flaked (sliced) hazelnuts.

Apple, Apricot and Walnut Loaf

Serve warm and store what is left in an airtight tin.

Makes 1 loaf
225g/8oz/2 cups plain (all-purpose)
wholemeal (whole-wheat) flour
5ml/1 tsp baking powder
pinch of salt
115g/4oz/½ cup sunflower margarine
175g/6oz/¾ cup soft light brown sugar
2 eggs, lightly beaten
grated rind and juice of 1 orange
50g/2oz/½ cup chopped walnuts
50g/2oz/¼ cup ready-to-eat dried
apricots, chopped
1 large cooking apple

1 Preheat the oven to 180°C/350°F/
Gas 4. Grease and line a 900g/2lb loaf
tin (pan).

3 Stir in the walnuts and apricots. Peel,
quarter, and core the apple, chop it
roughly and add it to the mixture. Stir,
then spoon into the prepared tin and level
the top.

4 Bake for 1 hour, or until a skewer
inserted into the centre of the loaf
comes out clean. Cool in the tin for about
5 minutes, then turn the loaf out on to a
wire rack and peel off the lining paper.

NUTRITION NOTES
Per portion (serves 10–12)

Energy	290Kcals/1220kJ
Fat	14.5g
Saturated Fat	2.5g
Cholesterol	43.5mg
Fibre	1.6g

2 Sift the flour, baking powder and salt
into a large mixing bowl, then tip
the bran remaining in the sieve into the
mixture. Add the margarine, sugar, eggs,
orange rind and juice. Stir, then beat with
a hand-held electric beater until smooth.

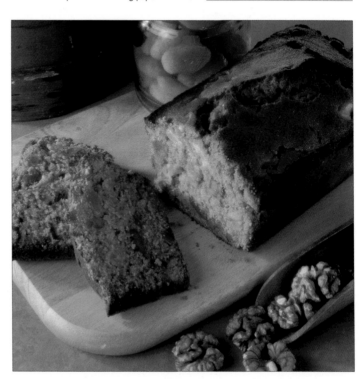

Banana and Ginger Teabread

Serve this teabread in slices with low-fat spread. The stem ginger adds an interesting flavour.

Makes 1 loaf
175g/6oz/1½ cups self-raising (self-rising) flour
5ml/1 tsp baking powder
40g/1½oz/3 tbsp soft margarine
50g/2oz/¼ cup dark muscovado (molasses) sugar
50g/2oz/¼ cup drained stem ginger, chopped
60ml/4 tbsp skimmed milk
2 ripe bananas, mashed

NUTRITION NOTES

Per portion (serves 6–8)

Energy	214Kcals/899kJ
Fat	5.16g
Saturated Fat	0.96g
Cholesterol	0.57mg
Fibre	1.59g

1 Preheat the oven to 180°C/350°F/ Gas 4. Grease and line a 450g/1lb loaf tin (pan). Sift the flour and baking powder into a mixing bowl.

2 Rub in the margarine until the mixture resembles breadcrumbs.

3 Stir in the sugar. Add the ginger, milk and bananas and mix to a soft dough.

4 Spoon into the prepared tin and bake for 40–45 minutes, or until a skewer inserted into the centre comes out clean. Run a metal spatula around the edges to loosen, then turn the teabread on to a wire rack and leave to cool.

Glazed Banana Spice Loaf

For an instant variation, omit the glaze and spread with quark for a tea-time treat.

1 Preheat the oven to 180°C/350°F/
Gas 4. Line a 23 x 13cm/9 x 5in loaf
tin (pan) with greased baking parchment.

2 With a fork, mash the banana in a
bowl. Set aside.

3 With an electric mixer, cream the
butter and sugar until light and fluffy.
Add the eggs, one at a time, beating to
blend well after each addition. Sift
together the flour, salt, bicarbonate of
soda, nutmeg, allspice and cloves. Add to
the butter mixture and stir to combine well.

4 Add the sour cream, banana and
vanilla essence and mix just enough
to blend. Pour into the prepared tin.

5 Bake for 45–50 minutes, until the top
springs back when touched lightly.
Allow to cool in the tin for 10 minutes
before turning out on to a wire rack.

6 For the glaze, combine the icing sugar
and lemon juice, then stir until
smooth. To glaze, set the rack over a
baking sheet. Pour the glaze over the top
of the bread and allow to set.

Makes 1 loaf

1 large ripe banana
115g/4oz/½ cup butter
175g/6oz/scant 1 cup granulated sugar
2 eggs
175g/6oz/1½ cups plain (all-purpose) flour
5ml/1 tsp salt
5ml/1 tsp bicarbonate of soda
(baking soda)
2.5ml/½ tsp freshly grated nutmeg
1.5ml/¼ tsp ground allspice
1.5ml/¼ tsp ground cloves
150ml/¼ pint/⅔ cup sour cream
5ml/1 tsp vanilla essence (extract)

For the glaze

175g/6oz/1 cup icing
(confectioners') sugar
15–30ml/1–2 tbsp lemon juice

NUTRITION NOTES

Per portion (serves 10)

Energy	362Kcals/1522kJ
Fat	14.1g
Saturated Fat	4.3g
Cholesterol	49mg
Fibre	0.8g

Orange Honey Bread

A moist and fruity bread using naturally sweet ingredients.

Makes 1 loaf

275g/10oz/2½ cups plain (all-purpose) flour
12.5ml/2½ tsp baking powder
2.5ml/½ tsp bicarbonate of soda
(baking soda)
2.5ml/½ tsp salt
30ml/2 tbsp margarine
350g/12oz/1¼ cups clear honey
1 egg, lightly beaten
25ml/1½ tbsp grated orange rind
175ml/6fl oz/¾ cup freshly squeezed
orange juice
75g/3oz/¾ cups chopped walnuts

NUTRITION NOTES

Per portion (serves 10)

Energy	300Kcals/1257kJ
Fat	11.2g
Saturated Fat	1.49g
Cholesterol	19.5mg
Fibre	1.6g

1 Preheat the oven to 160°C/325°F/ Gas 3. Sift together the flour, baking powder, bicarbonate of soda and salt.

2 Line the bottom and sides of a 23 x 13cm/9 x 5in loaf tin (pan) with greased baking parchment.

3 With an electric mixer, cream the margarine until soft. Stir in the honey until blended, then stir in the egg. Add the orange rind and stir to combine.

4 Fold the flour mixture into the honey and egg mixture in three batches, alternating with the orange juice. Stir in the walnuts.

5 Pour into the tin and bake for 60–70 minutes, or until a skewer inserted into the centre comes out clean. Allow to stand for 10 minutes before turning on to a rack to cool.

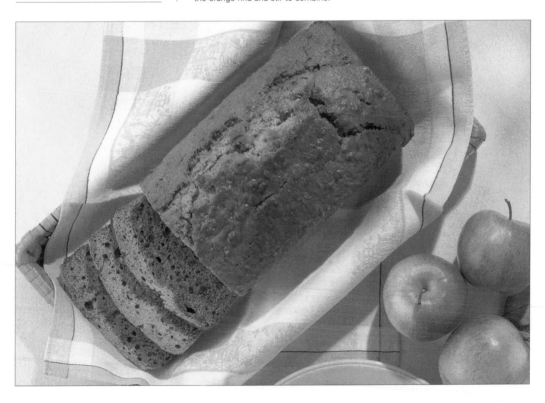

Apple-sauce Bread

Apples and spices such as cinnamon and nutmeg are a match made in heaven.

1 Preheat the oven to 180°C/350°F/ Gas 4. Line the bottom and sides of a 23 x 13cm/9 x 5in loaf tin (pan) with greased baking parchment.

2 Break the egg into a bowl and beat lightly. Stir in the stewed apple, butter or margarine, and both sugars. Set aside.

3 In another bowl, sift together the flour, baking powder, bicarbonate of soda, salt, cinnamon and nutmeg. Fold the dry ingredients into the apple sauce mixture in three batches.

4 Stir in the currants or raisins and chopped pecan nuts.

5 Pour into the prepared tin and bake for about 1 hour, or until a skewer inserted in the centre comes out clean. Leave to stand for 10 minutes before transferring to a cooling rack.

Makes 1 loaf

1 egg
225g/8oz/1 cup stewed apple
50g/2oz/¼ cup butter or margarine, melted
75g/3oz/⅓ cup soft dark brown sugar
50g/2oz/¼ cup granulated sugar
225g/8oz/2 cups plain (all-purpose) flour
10ml/2 tsp baking powder
2.5ml/½ tsp bicarbonate of soda (baking soda)
2.5ml/½ tsp salt
5ml/1 tsp ground cinnamon
2.5ml/½ tsp freshly grated nutmeg
75g/3oz/½ cup currants or raisins
175g/6oz/1 cup pecan nuts, chopped

NUTRITION NOTES
Per portion (serves 10)

Energy	299Kcals/1255kJ
Fat	11.2g
Saturated Fat	1.2g
Cholesterol	20mg
Fibre	1.8g

Cranberry Orange Bread

Try this classic muffin combination in a tasty teabread.

Makes 1 loaf

225g/8oz/2 cups plain (all-purpose) flour
115g/4oz/generous ½ cup caster (superfine) sugar
15ml/1 tbsp baking powder
2.5ml/½ tsp salt
grated rind of 1 large orange
150ml/¼ pint/⅔ cup fresh orange juice
2 eggs, lightly beaten
75g/3oz/6 tbsp butter or margarine, melted
175g/6oz/1½ cups fresh cranberries
50g/2oz/½ cup walnuts, chopped

NUTRITION NOTES

Per portion (serves 10)

Energy	285Kcals/1195kJ
Fat	14g
Saturated Fat	2.3g
Cholesterol	39mg
Fibre	2g

1 Preheat the oven to 180°C/350°F/ Gas 4. Line the bottom and sides of a 23 x 13cm/9 x 5in loaf tin (pan) with greased baking parchment. Sift the flour, sugar, baking powder and salt into a bowl.

2 Stir the grated orange rind into the dry ingredients.

3 Make a well in the centre of the dry ingredients and add the orange juice, eggs and melted butter or margarine. Stir from the centre until the ingredients are blended; do not overmix.

4 Add the cranberries and walnuts and stir well until blended. Transfer the batter to the prepared tin and bake for 45–50 minutes, or until a skewer inserted in the centre comes out clean.

5 Leave to cool in the tin for about 10 minutes before transferring to a rack to cool completely. Serve thinly sliced, toasted or plain, with butter or cream cheese and jam.

Pear Teabread

This is an ideal teabread to make when pears are plentiful – an excellent use for windfalls.

1 Preheat the oven to 180°C/350°F/ Gas 4. Grease and line a 450g/1lb loaf tin (pan) with baking parchment. Put the oats in a bowl with the sugar, pour over the pear or apple juice and oil, mix well and leave to stand for 15 minutes.

2 Quarter, core and coarsely grate the pears. Add the fruit to the oat mixture with the flour, sultanas, baking powder, mixed spice and egg, then mix together thoroughly.

3 Spoon the mixture into the prepared loaf tin and level the top. Bake for 50–60 minutes or until a skewer inserted into the centre comes out clean.

4 Transfer the teabread to a wire rack and peel off the lining paper. Leave to cool completely.

Cook's Tip
Health food shops sell concentrated pear and apple juice, ready for diluting as required.

Makes 1 loaf
25g/1oz/¼ cup rolled oats
50g/2oz/¼ cup light muscovado (brown) sugar
30ml/2 tbsp pear or apple juice
30ml/2 tbsp sunflower oil
1 large or 2 small pears
115g/4oz/1 cup self-raising flour
115g/4oz/⅔ cup sultanas (golden raisins)
2.5ml/½ tsp baking powder
10ml/2 tsp mixed (apple pie) spice
1 egg

NUTRITION NOTES
Per portion (serves 6–8)
Energy	200Kcals/814kJ
Fat	4.61g
Saturated Fat	0.79g
Cholesterol	27.5mg
Fibre	1.39g

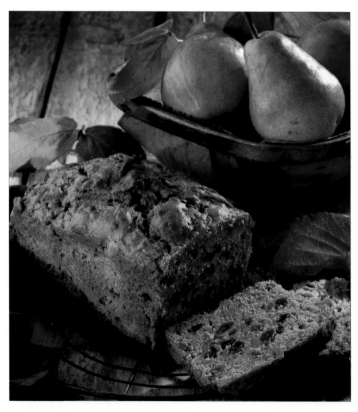

Dried Fruit Loaf

Dried fruit is a healthy sweet treat, and delicious in this loaf.

Makes 1 loaf
425g/15oz/2½ cups mixed dried fruit,
such as currants, raisins,
chopped dried apricots and
dried cherries
300ml/½ pint/1¼ cups cold strong
black tea
175g/6oz/¾ cup soft dark brown sugar
grated rind and juice of 1 small orange
grated rind and juice of 1 lemon
1 egg, lightly beaten
200g/7oz/1¾ cups plain (all-purpose) flour
15ml/1 tbsp baking powder
0.75ml/⅛ tsp salt

NUTRITION NOTES
Per portion (serves 10)

Energy	298Kcals/1252kJ
Fat	1.1g
Saturated Fat	0.2g
Cholesterol	19.2mg
Fibre	1.8g

1 In a bowl, toss together all the dried fruit, pour over the tea and leave to soak overnight.

2 Preheat the oven to 180°C/350°F/ Gas 4. Line the bottom and sides of a 23 x 13cm/9 x 5in loaf tin (pan) with greased baking parchment.

3 Strain the fruit, reserving the liquid. In a bowl, combine the sugar, orange and lemon rind and fruit.

4 Pour the orange and lemon juice into a measuring cup; if the quantity is less than 250ml/8fl oz/1 cup, make up with the soaking liquid.

5 Stir the citrus juices and egg into the dried fruit mixture.

6 In another bowl, sift together the flour, baking powder and salt. Stir into the fruit mixture until blended.

7 Transfer to the prepared tin and bake for 1¼ hours, or until a skewer inserted in the centre comes out clean. Allow to stand for 10 minutes before turning out.

Date and Nut Malt Loaf

A moist loaf – perfect for packed lunches.

1 Sift the flours and salt into a large bowl, adding any bran from the sieve. Stir in the sugar and yeast.

2 Put the butter or margarine in a small pan with the treacle and malt extract. Stir over a low heat until melted. Leave to cool, then combine with the milk.

3 Stir the liquid into the dry ingredients and knead thoroughly for 15 minutes until the dough is elastic. (If you have a dough blade on your food processor, follow the manufacturer's instructions for exact timings.)

4 Knead in the fruits and nuts. Transfer the dough to an oiled bowl, cover with clear film (plastic wrap), and leave in a warm place for about 1½ hours, until the dough has doubled in size.

5 Grease two 450g/1lb loaf tins (pans). Knock back (punch down) the dough and knead lightly. Divide in half, form into loaves and place in the tins. Cover and leave in a warm place for about 30 minutes, until risen. Meanwhile, preheat the oven to 190°C/ 375°F/Gas 5.

6 Bake for 35–40 minutes, until well risen and sounding hollow when tapped underneath. Cool on a wire rack. Brush with 30ml/2 tbsp clear honey while warm to glaze, if you wish.

Makes 2 loaves

300g/11oz/2⅔ cups strong white bread flour
275g/10oz/2½ cups strong wholemeal (whole-wheat) bread flour
5ml/1 tsp salt
75g/3oz/⅓ cup soft brown sugar
15ml/1 tsp easy-blend (rapid-rise) dried yeast
50g/2oz/¼ cup butter or margarine
15ml/1 tbsp black treacle (molasses)
60ml/4 tbsp malt extract
scant 250ml/8fl oz/1 cup tepid milk
115g/4oz/½ cup chopped dates
75g/3oz/½ cup sultanas (golden raisins)
75g/3oz/⅔ cup raisins
50g/2oz/½ cup chopped nuts

NUTRITION NOTES

Per portion (serves 12)

Energy	216Kcals/907kJ
Fat	5.57g
Saturated Fat	2.46g
Cholesterol	9.45mg
Fibre	2.8g

Malt Loaf

This is a rich and sticky loaf. If it lasts long enough to go stale, try toasting it for a delicious tea-time treat.

Makes 1 loaf
about 150ml/¼ pint/⅔ cup warm skimmed milk
5ml/1 tsp dried yeast
pinch of caster (superfine) sugar
350g/12oz/3 cups plain (all-purpose) flour
1.5ml/½ tsp salt
30ml/2 tbsp light muscovado (brown) sugar
175g/6oz/1 cup sultanas (golden raisins)
15ml/1 tbsp sunflower oil
45ml/3 tbsp malt extract

For the glaze
30ml/2 tbsp caster (superfine) sugar
30ml/2 tbsp water

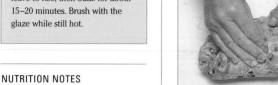

Cook's Tip
To make buns, divide the dough into ten pieces, shape into rounds, leave to rise, then bake for about 15–20 minutes. Brush with the glaze while still hot.

NUTRITION NOTES
Per portion (serves 8)

Energy	279Kcals/1171kJ
Fat	2.06g
Saturated Fat	0.33g
Cholesterol	0.38mg
Fibre	1.79g

1 Place the warm milk in a bowl. Sprinkle the yeast on top and add the sugar. Leave for 30 minutes until frothy. Stir the flour and salt into a mixing bowl, stir in the muscovado sugar and sultanas, and make a well in the centre.

2 Add the yeast mixture with the oil and malt extract. Gradually incorporate the flour and mix to a soft dough, adding a little extra milk if necessary.

3 Turn on to a floured surface and knead for about 5 minutes until smooth and elastic. Grease a 450g/1lb loaf tin (pan).

4 Shape the dough and place it in the prepared loaf tin. Cover with a damp dishtowel and leave in a warm place for about 1–2 hours until the dough is well risen. Preheat the oven to 190°C/375°F/Gas 5.

5 Bake the loaf for 30–35 minutes, or until it sounds hollow when it is tapped underneath.

6 Meanwhile, prepare the glaze by dissolving the sugar in the water in a small pan. Bring to the boil, stirring, then lower the heat and simmer for 1 minute. Place the loaf on a wire rack and brush with the glaze while still hot. Leave the loaf to cool before serving.

Lemon Walnut Bread

This is a light and tangy teabread.

Makes 1 loaf

115g/4oz/½ cup butter or margarine
115g/4oz/generous ½ cup caster
(superfine) sugar
2 eggs, separated
grated rind of 2 lemons
30ml/2 tbsp fresh lemon juice
175g/6oz/1½ cups self-raising
(self-rising) flour
10ml/2 tsp baking powder
120ml/4fl oz/½ cup milk
175g/6oz/1½ cups chopped walnuts
0.75ml/⅛ tsp salt

NUTRITION NOTES

Per portion (serves 10)

Energy	229Kcals/962kJ
Fat	11.1g
Saturated Fat	1.77g
Cholesterol	39.1mg
Fibre	1g

1 Preheat the oven to 180°C/350°F/ Gas 4. Line the bottom and sides of a 23 x 13cm/9 x 5in loaf tin (pan) with baking parchment and grease.

2 With an electric mixer, cream the butter or margarine with the sugar until light and fluffy.

3 Beat the egg yolks into the creamed butter and sugar.

4 Add the lemon rind and juice and stir until blended. Set aside.

5 In another bowl, sift together the flour and baking powder, three times. Fold into the butter mixture in three batches, alternating with the milk. Fold in the chopped walnuts and set the mixture aside.

6 Beat the egg whites and salt until stiff peaks form. Fold a large dollop of the egg whites into the walnut mixture to lighten it. Fold in the remaining egg whites carefully until just blended.

7 Pour the batter into the prepared tin and bake for 45–50 minutes, or until a skewer inserted in the centre of the loaf comes out clean. Leave to stand for 5 minutes before turning on to a rack to cool completely.

Apricot Nut Loaf

An excellent high-fibre fruit and nut combination.

1 Preheat the oven to 180°C/350°F/ Gas 4. Line the bottom and sides of a 23 x 13cm/9 x 5in loaf tin (pan) with baking parchment and grease.

2 Place the apricots in a bowl and add lukewarm water to cover. Allow to stand for 30 minutes.

9 Stir in the walnuts. Spoon the batter into the prepared tin and bake for about 55–60 minutes, or until a skewer inserted in the centre of the loaf comes out clean. If the loaf browns too quickly, protect the top with foil. Cool in the tin for 10 minutes before transferring to a rack to cool completely.

3 With a vegetable peeler, remove the orange rind, leaving the pith.

4 With a sharp knife, finely chop the orange rind strips.

5 Drain the apricots and chop coarsely. Place in a bowl with the orange rind and raisins. Set aside.

6 Squeeze the peeled orange. Measure the juice and add enough hot water to make 175ml/6fl oz/¾ cup liquid.

7 Pour the orange juice mixture over the apricot mixture. Stir in the sugar, oil and eggs. Set aside.

8 In another bowl, sift together the flour, baking powder, salt and bicarbonate of soda. Fold the flour mixture into the apricot mixture in three batches.

Makes 1 loaf

175g/6oz/¾ cup dried apricots
1 large orange
75g/3oz/⅔ cup raisins
150g/5oz/¾ cup caster (superfine) sugar
90ml/3fl oz/⅓ cup oil
2 eggs, lightly beaten
250g/9oz/2¼ cups plain (all-purpose) flour
10ml/2 tsp baking powder
2.5ml/½ tsp salt
5ml/1 tsp bicarbonate soda (baking soda)
50g/2oz/½ cup chopped walnuts

NUTRITION NOTES

Per portion (serves 10)

Energy	324Kcals/1365kJ
Fat	11.2g
Saturated Fat	1.5g
Cholesterol	38mg
Fibre	2.5g

Date-nut Bread

A little brandy gives this teabread an extra rich flavour.

Makes 1 loaf
150g/5oz/1¼ cups pitted dates, chopped
175ml/6fl oz/¾ cup boiling water
60ml/4 tbsp unsalted (sweet) butter
40g/1½oz/scant ¼ cup soft dark
brown sugar
50g/2oz/¼ cup caster (superfine) sugar
1 egg
30ml/2 tbsp brandy
165g/5½oz/1⅓ cups plain
(all-purpose) flour
10ml/2 tsp baking powder
2.5ml/½ tsp salt
generous 2.5ml/½ tsp freshly
grated nutmeg
75g/3oz/¾ cup pecan nuts,
coarsely chopped

NUTRITION NOTES
Per portion (serves 10)

Energy	258Kcals/1077kJ
Fat	13.8g
Saturated Fat	1.1g
Cholesterol	20mg
Fibre	1.3g

1 Place the dates in a bowl and pour over the boiling water. Set aside to cool until lukewarm.

2 Preheat the oven to 180°C/350°F/ Gas 4. Line the bottom and sides of a 23 x 13cm/9 x 5in loaf tin (pan) with baking parchment and grease.

3 With an electric mixer, cream the butter and sugars until they are light and fluffy. Beat in the egg and brandy, then set aside.

4 Sift the flour, baking powder, salt and nutmeg together, three times.

5 Fold the dry ingredients into the sugar mixture in three batches, alternating with the dates and water.

6 Fold in the pecan nuts. Pour the batter into the prepared tin and bake for 45–50 minutes, or until a skewer inserted in the centre comes out clean. Cool in the pan for 10 minutes before transferring to a rack to cool completely.

Prune Bread

A slightly spicy bread that tastes good with savoury spreads.

1 Simmer the prunes in water to cover until soft, or soak overnight. Drain, reserving 50ml/2fl oz/¼ cup of the soaking liquid. Pit and chop the prunes.

2 Combine the yeast and the reserved prune liquid, stir, and leave for 15 minutes to dissolve.

3 In a large bowl, stir together the flours, bicarbonate of soda, salt and pepper. Make a well in the centre.

4 Add the chopped prunes, butter and buttermilk. Pour in the yeast mixture. With a wooden spoon, stir from the centre, incorporating more flour with each turn, to obtain a rough dough.

5 Transfer to a floured surface and knead until smooth and elastic. Return to the clean bowl, cover with a plastic bag, and leave to rise in a warm place until doubled in volume, for about 1½ hours. Grease a baking sheet.

6 Knock back (punch down) the dough with your fist, then knead in the chopped walnuts.

7 Shape the dough into a long, cylindrical loaf. Place on the baking sheet, cover loosely, and leave to rise in a warm place for 45 minutes.

8 Preheat the oven to 220°C/425°F/Gas 7. With a sharp knife, score the top deeply. Brush with milk and bake for 15 minutes. Lower the heat to 190°C/375°F/Gas 5 and bake for 35 minutes more, until the bottom sounds hollow when tapped. Cool on a rack.

Makes 1 loaf

225g/8oz/1 cup prunes
10ml/2 tsp dried yeast
50g/2oz/½ cup strong wholemeal (whole-wheat) bread flour
275–350g/10–12oz/2½–3 cups strong white bread flour
2.5ml/½ tsp bicarbonate of soda (baking soda)
5ml/1 tsp salt
5ml/1 tsp ground black pepper
30ml/2 tbsp butter
175ml/6fl oz/¾ cup buttermilk
175g/6oz/1 cup walnuts, chopped

NUTRITION NOTES

Per portion (serves 10)

Energy	262Kcals/1104kJ
Fat	8.4g
Saturated Fat	1.1g
Cholesterol	1mg
Fibre	2.1g

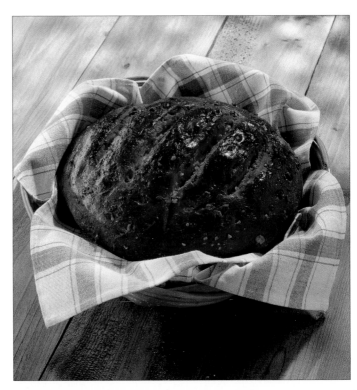

Swedish Fruit Bread

A lightly sweetened fruit bread that is delicious served warm. It is also excellent toasted and topped with low-fat spread.

Makes 1 loaf

150ml/¼ pint/⅔ cup lukewarm water
5ml/1 tsp dried yeast
15ml/1 tbsp clear honey
225g/8oz/2 cups strong wholemeal (whole-wheat) bread flour
225g/8oz/2 cups strong white bread flour
5ml/1 tsp salt
115g/4oz/⅔ cup sultanas (golden raisins)
50g/2oz/⅓ cup walnuts, finely chopped
175ml/6fl oz/¾ cup warm skimmed milk, plus extra for glazing

Variation

To make Apple and Hazelnut Bread, replace the sultanas with two chopped eating apples and use chopped toasted hazelnuts instead of the walnuts. Add 5ml/1 tsp ground cinnamon with the flour.

NUTRITION NOTES

Per portion (serves 8–10)

Energy	273Kcals/1145kJ
Fat	4.86g
Saturated Fat	0.57g
Cholesterol	0.39mg
Fibre	3.83g

1 Put the water in a small jug. Sprinkle the yeast on top. Add a few drops of the honey to help activate the yeast, mix well and leave to stand for 10 minutes.

2 Put the flours in a mixing bowl, with the salt and sultanas. Set aside 15ml/1 tbsp of the walnuts and add the rest to the bowl. Mix together lightly and make a well in the centre.

3 Add the yeast and honey mixture to the flour mixture with the milk and remaining honey. Gradually incorporate the flour, mixing to a soft dough; add a little extra water if the dough feels too dry to work with.

4 Turn the dough on to a floured surface and knead for 5 minutes until smooth and elastic. Return to the clean bowl, cover with a damp dishtowel and leave in a warm place to rise for about 2 hours until doubled in bulk. Grease a baking sheet.

5 Turn the dough on to a floured surface and form into a 28cm/11in long sausage shape. Place on the baking sheet. Make some diagonal cuts down the whole length of the loaf.

6 Brush the loaf with milk, sprinkle with the reserved walnuts and leave to rise for about 40 minutes. Preheat the oven to 220°C/425°F/Gas 7. Bake for 10 minutes. Lower the temperature to 200°C/400°F/Gas 6 and bake for about 20 minutes more, or until the loaf sounds hollow when tapped.

Raisin Bread

Spice, brandy and dried fruit make a good flavour combination.

Makes 2 loaves

10ml/2 tsp dried yeast
475ml/16fl oz/2 cups lukewarm milk
175g/6oz/1¼ cups raisins
65g/2½oz/¼ cup currants
15ml/1 tbsp sherry or brandy
2.5ml/½ tsp freshly grated nutmeg
grated rind of 1 large orange
75g/3oz/6 tbsp caster (superfine) sugar
15ml/1 tbsp salt
115g/4oz/½ cup butter, melted
500–675g/1¼–1½lb/5–6 cups
strong white bread flour
1 egg beaten with 15ml/1 tbsp cream,
to glaze

NUTRITION NOTES

Per portion (serves 20)

Energy	235Kcals/994kJ
Fat	5.9g
Saturated Fat	1.2g
Cholesterol	11mg
Fibre	1.4g

1 Stir together the yeast and 120ml/4fl oz/½ cup of the milk and let stand for 15 minutes to dissolve.

2 Mix the raisins, currants, sherry or brandy, nutmeg and orange rind together and set aside.

3 In another bowl, mix the remaining milk, sugar, salt and 50g/2oz/¼ cup of the butter. Add the yeast mixture. With a wooden spoon, stir in 225–275g/8–10oz/2–3 cups flour, 115g/4oz/1 cup at a time, until blended. Add more flour for a stiff dough.

4 Transfer to a floured surface and knead until smooth and elastic. Place in a greased bowl, cover, and leave to rise in a warm place until doubled in volume, for about 2½ hours.

5 Knock back (punch down) the dough, return to the bowl, cover, and leave to rise in a warm place for about 30 minutes.

6 Grease two 23 x 13cm/9 x 5in bread tins (pans). Divide the dough in half and roll each half into a rectangle about 50 x 18cm/20 x 7in.

7 Brush the rectangles with the remaining melted butter. Sprinkle over the raising mixture, then roll up tightly from the short end, tucking in the ends slightly as you roll. Place in the prepared tins, cover and leave to rise until almost doubled in volume.

8 Preheat the oven to 200°C/400°F/Gas 6. Brush the top of the loaves with the glaze. Bake for 20 minutes. Lower the heat to 180°C/350°F/Gas 4 and bake for 25–30 minutes more, or until golden. Cool on racks.

Sweet Potato and Raisin Bread

The natural sweetness of sweet potato is used in this healthy loaf.

1 Preheat the oven to 180°C/350°F/ Gas 4. Grease a 23 x 13cm/9 x 5in loaf tin (pan).

2 Sift the flour, baking powder, salt, cinnamon and nutmeg into a small bowl. Set aside.

5 Transfer the batter to the prepared tin. Bake for 1–1¼ hours, or until a skewer inserted in the centre comes out clean.

6 Cool in the pan on a wire rack for 15 minutes, then turn the bread on to a wire rack and cool completely.

Makes 1 loaf
225–275g/8–10oz/2–2½ cups plain (all-purpose) flour
10ml/2 tsp baking powder
2.5ml/½ tsp salt
5ml/1 tsp ground cinnamon
2.5ml/½ tsp freshly grated nutmeg
450g/1lb/5 cups cooked mashed sweet potatoes
75g/3oz/⅓ cup soft light brown sugar
115g/4oz/½ cup butter or margarine, melted and cooled
3 eggs, beaten
75g/3oz/generous ½ cup raisins

NUTRITION NOTES
Per portion (serves 10)
Energy	338Kcals/1420kJ
Fat	11.6g
Saturated Fat	2.4g
Cholesterol	59mg
Fibre	2.4g

3 With an electric mixer, beat the mashed sweet potatoes with the brown sugar, butter or margarine and eggs until well mixed.

4 Add the flour mixture and the raisins. Stir with a wooden spoon until the flour is just mixed in.

Cardamom and Saffron Tealoaf

An aromatic sweet bread ideal for afternoon tea or lightly toasted for breakfast. Using the sachets
of fast-action or easy-blend yeasts makes bread-making so simple.

Makes 1 loaf
good pinch of saffron threads
750ml/1¼ pints/3 cups lukewarm milk
25g/1oz/2 tbsp butter
900g/2lb/8 cups strong white bread flour
10ml/2 tsp easy-blend (rapid-rise)
dried yeast
40g/1½oz caster (superfine) sugar
6 cardamom pods, split open and
seeds extracted
115g/4oz/⅔ cup raisins
30ml/2 tbsp clear honey
1 egg, beaten

NUTRITION NOTES
Per portion (serves 20)

Energy	226Kcals/952kJ
Fat	2.1g
Saturated Fat	0.4g
Cholesterol	10mg
Fibre	1.7g

1 Crush the saffron into a cup containing a little of the warm milk and leave to infuse for 5 minutes.

2 Rub the butter into the flour, then mix in the yeast, sugar and cardamom seeds (these may need rubbing to separate them). Stir in the raisins.

3 Beat the remaining milk with the honey and egg, then mix this into the flour with the saffron milk and threads, stirring well until a firm dough is formed. You may not need all the milk; it depends on the flour.

4 Turn out the dough and knead it on a lightly floured board for about 5 minutes until smooth.

5 Return the dough to the mixing bowl, cover with oiled clear film (plastic wrap) and leave in a warm place until doubled in size. This should take between 1 and 3 hours. Grease a 900g/2lb loaf tin (pan). Turn the dough out on to a floured board again, knock it back (punch it down), knead for three minutes, then shape it into a fat roll and fit it into the greased loaf tin.

6 Cover with a sheet of lightly oiled clear film and stand in a warm place until the dough begins to rise again. Preheat the oven to 200°C/400°F/Gas 6. Bake the loaf for 25 minutes until golden brown and firm on top. Turn out of the tin and, as it cools, brush the top with honey. Slice when cold and spread with butter. It is also good lightly toasted.

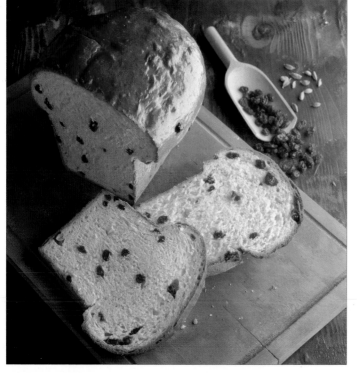

Sweet Sesame Loaf

Toasted sesame seeds add a lovely nutty flavour to this loaf.

1 Preheat the oven to 180°C/350°F/ Gas 4. Line a 25 x 15cm/10 x 6in baking tin (pan), or two small loaf tins (pans), with greased baking parchment.

5 Pour into the pan and sprinkle over the reserved sesame seeds.

6 Bake for about 1 hour, or until a skewer inserted into the centre comes out clean. Cool in the pan for 10 minutes before turning out.

2 Reserve 30ml/2 tbsp of the sesame seeds. Spread the rest on a baking sheet and bake until lightly toasted, for about 10 minutes. Sift the flour, baking powder and salt into a bowl.

Makes 1 large or 2 small loaves
150g/5oz/1¼ cups sesame seeds
225g/8oz/2 cups plain (all-purpose) flour
12.5ml/2½ tsp baking powder
5ml/1 tsp salt
60ml/4 tbsp butter or margarine
150g/5oz/¾ cup caster
(superfine) sugar
2 eggs
grated rind of 1 lemon
350ml/12fl oz/1½ cups milk

NUTRITION NOTES
Per portion (serves 10)

Energy	133Kcals/562kJ
Fat	5.1g
Saturated Fat	0.9g
Cholesterol	20mg
Fibre	0.7g

3 Stir in the toasted sesame seeds and set aside. With an electric mixer, cream the butter or margarine and sugar together until light and fluffy. Beat in the eggs, then stir in the lemon rind and milk.

4 Pour the milk mixture over the dry ingredients and fold in with a large metal spoon until just blended.

Greek Easter Bread

In Greece, Easter celebrations are very important, and involve much preparation in the kitchen. This bread is sold in all the bakers' shops, and is also made at home. It is traditionally decorated with red dyed eggs.

Makes 1 loaf
25g/1oz fresh yeast
120ml/4fl oz/½ cup warm milk
675g/1½lb/6 cups strong white
bread flour
2 eggs, beaten
2.5ml/½ tsp caraway seeds
15ml/1 tbsp caster (superfine) sugar
15ml/1 tbsp brandy
50g/2oz/¼ cup butter, melted
1 egg white, beaten
50g/2oz/½ cup split almonds
2–3 hard-boiled eggs, dyed red

NUTRITION NOTES
Per portion (serves 10)

Energy	344Kcals/1453kJ
Fat	10.1g
Saturated Fat	3.6g
Cholesterol	89mg
Fibre	2.5g

1 Crumble the yeast into a bowl. Mix with 15–30ml/1–2 tbsp of warm water, until softened. Add the milk and 115g/4oz/1 cup of the flour and mix to a creamy consistency. Cover with a cloth, and leave in a warm place to rise for 1 hour.

2 Sift the remaining flour into a large bowl and make a well in the centre. Pour the risen yeast into the well, and draw in a little of the flour from the sides. Add the eggs, caraway seeds, sugar and brandy. Incorporate the remaining flour until the mixture begins to form a dough.

3 Mix in the melted butter. Turn on to a floured surface and knead for about 10 minutes, until the dough becomes smooth. Return to the bowl and cover with a damp dishtowel. Leave in a warm place for 3 hours.

4 Preheat the oven to 180°C/350°F/Gas 4. Knock back (punch down) the dough, turn on to a floured surface and knead for a minute or two. Divide the dough into three and roll each piece into a long sausage shape. Make a braid as shown above and place the loaf on a greased baking sheet.

5 Tuck the ends under, brush with the egg white and decorate with the split almonds. Bake for about 1 hour, until the loaf sounds hollow when tapped underneath. Cool on a wire rack. Serve decorated with the hard-boiled eggs.

Orange Wheat Loaf

Perfect just with butter as a breakfast bread or teabread and lovely for banana sandwiches.

1 Sift the flour into a large bowl and return any wheat flakes from the sieve. Add the salt and rub in the butter lightly with your fingertips.

5 Bake the bread for 30–35 minutes, or until it sounds hollow when you tap the loaf underneath. Tip out of the tin and cool on a wire rack.

Makes 1 loaf
275g/10 oz/2½ cups plain (all-purpose) wholemeal (whole-wheat) flour
2.5ml/½ tsp salt
50g/2oz/¼ cup butter
25g/1oz/2 tbsp soft light brown sugar
½ sachet easy-blend (rapid-rise) dried yeast
grated rind and juice of ½ orange

NUTRITION NOTES
Per portion (serves 6–8)

Energy	144Kcals/607kJ
Fat	3.32g
Saturated Fat	1.82g
Cholesterol	7.19mg
Fibre	3.24g

2 Stir in the sugar, yeast and orange rind. Pour the orange juice into a measuring jug (cup) and make up to 200ml/7fl oz/scant 1 cup with hot water (the liquid should not be more than hand hot).

3 Stir the liquid into the flour and mix to a soft ball of dough. Knead the dough gently on a lightly floured surface until quite smooth.

4 Place the dough in a greased 450g/1lb loaf tin (pan) and leave in a warm place until nearly doubled in size. Preheat the oven to 220°C/425°F/Gas 7.

Baked
Savouries

Savouries cooked in the
oven, such as pizzas,
soufflés and tartlets, are
irresistible served warm
or piping hot. As an extra
bonus, popovers, parcels
and scones are also very
quick to make!

Smoked Salmon Pizzettes

Mini-pizzas topped with smoked salmon, crème fraîche and lumpfish roe make
an extra special party canapé.

Makes 10–12

150g/5oz packet of pizza dough mix
15ml/1 tbsp chopped
fresh chives
15ml/1 tbsp olive oil
75–115g/3–4oz smoked salmon,
cut into strips
60ml/4 tbsp crème fraîche
30ml/2 tbsp black lumpfish roe
chives, to garnish

NUTRITION NOTES

Per portion

Energy	126Kcals/532kJ
Fat	2.9g
Saturated Fat	0.8g
Cholesterol	37mg
Fibre	0.9g

1 Preheat the oven to 200°C/400°F/
Gas 6. Grease two baking sheets.
Knead the dough gently, adding the
chives until evenly mixed.

2 Roll out the dough on a lightly floured
surface to about 3mm/⅛in thick.
Using a 7.5cm/3in plain round cutter,
stamp out 10–12 rounds.

3 Place the bases well apart on the two
baking sheets, prick all over with a
fork, then brush with the oil. Bake for
10–15 minutes until crisp and golden.

4 Arrange the smoked salmon on top,
then spoon on the crème fraîche.
Spoon a tiny amount of lumpfish roe in
the centre and garnish with chives.
Serve immediately.

Calzone

Cut into this folded pizza to reveal a deliciously tempting filling.

1 To make the dough, sift the flour and salt into a bowl and stir in the yeast. Stir in just enough warm water to mix a soft dough.

2 Knead for 5 minutes until smooth. Cover and leave in a warm place for about 1 hour, or until doubled in size.

3 Meanwhile, to make the filling, heat the oil and sauté the onion and courgettes for 3–4 minutes. Remove from the heat and add the tomatoes, cheese, oregano and seasoning.

4 Preheat the oven to 220°C/425°F/ Gas 7. Knead the dough lightly and divide into four. Roll out each piece on a lightly floured surface to a 20cm/8in round and place a quarter of the filling on one half of each round.

5 Brush the edges with milk and fold over to enclose the filling. Press firmly to enclose. Brush with milk.

6 Bake on an oiled baking sheet for 15–20 minutes. Serve hot or cold.

Serves 4
450g/1lb/4 cups strong white bread flour
pinch of salt
10ml/2 tsp easy-blend (rapid-rise) dried yeast
350ml/12fl oz/1½ cups lukewarm water

For the filling
5ml/1 tsp olive oil
1 medium red onion, thinly sliced
3 medium courgettes (zucchini), sliced
2 large tomatoes, diced
150g/5oz mozzarella cheese, diced
15ml/1 tbsp chopped fresh oregano
salt and ground black pepper
skimmed milk, to glaze

NUTRITION NOTES
Per portion

Energy	544Kcals/2885kJ
Fat	10.93g
Saturated Fat	5.49g
Cholesterol	24.42mg
Fibre	5.09g

Fresh Herb Pizza

Cut this pizza into thin wedges and serve as part of a mixed antipasti.

Serves 8

115g/4oz mixed fresh herbs, such as
parsley, basil and oregano
3 garlic cloves, crushed
120ml/4fl oz/½ cup double (heavy) cream
1 pizza base, 25–30cm/
10–12in diameter
15ml/1 tbsp garlic oil
115g/4oz/1 cup grated Pecorino cheese
salt and ground black pepper

NUTRITION NOTES

Per portion

Energy	219Kcals/913kJ
Fat	8.1g
Saturated Fat	3.4g
Cholesterol	27mg
Fibre	1g

1 Preheat the oven to 220°C/425°F/ Gas 7. Chop the herbs, using a food processor if you have one.

2 In a bowl, mix together the herbs, garlic, cream and seasoning.

3 Brush the pizza base with the garlic oil, then spread over the herb and garlic mixture.

4 Sprinkle over the Pecorino cheese. Bake for 15–20 minutes until crisp and golden and the topping is still moist. Cut into thin wedges to serve.

Mini-pizzas

For a quick supper, try these delicious little pizzas made with fresh and sun-dried tomatoes.

Makes 4
150g/5oz packet of pizza dough mix
8 halves sun-dried tomatoes in olive
oil, drained
50g/2oz/½ cup pitted black olives
1 ripe beefsteak tomato, sliced
50g/2oz/¼ cup goat's cheese
30ml/2 tbsp fresh basil leaves

1 Preheat the oven to 200°C/400°F/ Gas 6. Make up the pizza base following the instructions on the side of the packet.

4 Top with the tomato slices and crumble over the goat's cheese. Bake for 10–15 minutes. Sprinkle with the fresh basil and serve at once.

NUTRITION NOTES
Per portion

Energy	326Kcals/1369kJ
Fat	11.3g
Saturated Fat	2.8g
Cholesterol	34mg
Fibre	2.8g

2 Divide the dough into four and roll each piece out to a 13cm/5in round. Place on two lightly oiled baking sheets.

3 Place the sun-dried tomatoes and olives in a blender or food processor and blend until smooth. Spread the mixture evenly over the pizza bases.

Cook's Tip
You could use loose sun-dried tomatoes (preserved without oil) instead. Leave in a bowl of warm water for 10–15 minutes to soften, drain and blend with the olives.

Spinach and Feta Triangles

Feta is a medium fat cheese and has a tangy flavour.

Makes 20

30ml/2 tbsp olive oil
2 shallots, finely chopped
450g/1lb/3 cups frozen
spinach, thawed
115g/4oz/1 cup crumbled feta cheese
25g/1oz/2 tbsp walnut pieces, chopped
1.5ml/¼ tsp freshly grated nutmeg
4 large or 8 small sheets filo pastry,
thawed if frozen
50g/2oz/¼ cup butter or
margarine, melted
salt and ground black pepper

Variation

For an alternative filling, omit the spinach and shallots. Use 350g/12oz/1½ cups crumbled goat's cheese, instead of the feta cheese, and 50g/2oz/½ cup toasted pine nuts instead of the walnuts. Mix the cheese with the olive oil and 15ml/1 tbsp chopped fresh basil. Assemble as above.

NUTRITION NOTES

Per portion

Energy	105Kcals/434J
Fat	9g
Saturated Fat	2g
Cholesterol	4mg
Fibre	0.6g

1 Preheat the oven to 200°C/400°F/ Gas 6.

2 Heat the olive oil in a skillet. Add the shallots and cook until softened, for about 5 minutes.

3 A handful at a time, squeeze all the liquid out of the spinach. Add the spinach to the shallots. Increase the heat to high and cook, stirring, until all the excess moisture has evaporated, for about 5 minutes.

4 Transfer the spinach mixture to a bowl. Cool. Stir in the feta and walnuts. Season with nutmeg, salt and pepper.

5 Lay a filo sheet on a flat surface. (Keep the remaining filo covered with a damp cloth to prevent it drying out.) Brush with some of the butter or margarine. Lay a second filo sheet on top of the first. With scissors, cut the layered filo pastry lengthways into 7.5cm/3in wide strips.

6 Place 15ml/1tbsp of the spinach mixture at the end of one strip of filo pastry.

7 Fold a bottom corner of the pastry over the filling to form a triangle, then continue folding over the pastry strip to the other end. Fill and shape the triangles until all the ingredients are used.

8 Set the triangles on baking sheets and brush with butter. Bake the filo triangles until they are crispy and golden brown, for about 10 minutes. Serve hot.

Salmon Parcels

Serve these little savoury parcels just as they are for a snack, or with a pool of fresh tomato sauce for a special starter.

Makes 12

90g/3½oz can red or pink salmon
15ml/1 tbsp chopped fresh
coriander (cilantro)
4 spring onions (scallions),
finely chopped
4 sheets filo pastry, thawed if frozen
sunflower oil, for brushing
spring onions (scallions) and salad
leaves, to serve

NUTRITION NOTES

Per portion
Energy	25Kcals/107kJ
Fat	1.16g
Saturated Fat	0.23g
Cholesterol	2.55mg
Fibre	0.05g

1 Preheat the oven to 200°C/400°F/ Gas 6. Lightly oil a baking sheet. Drain the salmon, discarding any skin and bones, then place in a bowl.

2 Flake the salmon with a fork and then mix with the fresh coriander and spring onions.

3 Place a single sheet of filo pastry on a work surface and brush lightly with oil. Then place another sheet on top. Cut into six squares, about 10cm/4in. Repeat with the remaining pastry, to make 12 squares.

4 Place a spoonful of the salmon mixture on to each square. Brush the edges of the pastry with oil, then draw together as shown above, pressing to seal. Place the pastries on a baking sheet and bake for 12–15 minutes, until golden. Serve warm, with spring onions and salad leaves.

Cook's Tip

When you are using filo pastry, it is important to prevent it drying out; cover any you are not using with a dishtowel or clear film (plastic wrap).

Tomato Cheese Tarts

These crisp little tartlets are easier to make than they look. They are best eaten fresh from the oven.

1 Preheat the oven to 200°C/400°F/ Gas 6. Brush the sheets of filo pastry lightly with egg white and cut into sixteen 10cm/4in squares.

3 Arrange tomatoes on the tarts, add seasoning and bake for 10–12 minutes, until golden. Serve warm.

Serves 4
2 sheets filo pastry, thawed if frozen
1 egg white
115g/4oz/½ cup skimmed-
milk soft cheese
handful of fresh basil leaves
3 small tomatoes, sliced
salt and ground black pepper

NUTRITION NOTES
Per portion

Energy	50Kcals/210kJ
Fat	0.33g
Saturated Fat	0.05g
Cholesterol	0.29mg
Fibre	0.25g

2 Layer the squares in twos, in eight patty tins (muffin pans). Spoon the cheese into the pastry cases. Season with black pepper and top with basil leaves.

Red Pepper and Watercress Filo Parcels

Peppery watercress combines well with sweet red pepper in these crisp little parcels.

Makes 8

3 red (bell) peppers
175g/6oz/1 bunch watercress or
rocket (arugula)
225g/8oz/1 cup ricotta cheese
50g/2oz/⅓ cup blanched almonds,
toasted and chopped
8 sheets filo pastry, thawed if frozen
30ml/2 tbsp olive oil
salt and ground black pepper

NUTRITION NOTES

Per portion
Energy   168Kcals/699kJ
Fat   10.2g
Saturated Fat   2.7g
Cholesterol   14mg
Fibre   1.7g

1 Preheat the oven to 190°C/375°F/ Gas 5. Place the peppers under a hot grill until blistered and charred. Place in a plastic bag. When cool enough to handle, peel, seed and pat dry on kitchen paper.

2 Place the peppers and watercress or rocket in a food processor and blend until coarsely chopped. Spoon into a bowl.

3 Mix in the ricotta and almonds, and season to taste.

4 Working with one sheet of filo pastry at a time, cut out two 18cm/7in and two 5cm/2in squares from each sheet. Brush one large square with a little olive oil and place a second large square at an angle of 90 degrees to form a star shape.

5 Place one of the small squares in the centre of the star shape, brush lightly with oil and top with a second small square.

6 Top with ⅛ of the red pepper mixture. Bring the edges together to form a purse shape and twist to seal. Place on a lightly greased baking sheet and cook for 25–30 minutes until golden.

Filo Clam Puffs

These mouthwatering bite-size parcels of seafood are ideal served as party nibbles with drinks.

Makes 54

9 sheets filo pastry, each about
30 x 45cm/12 x 18in, thawed if frozen
350g/12oz/1½ cups skimmed-
milk soft cheese
1 egg, beaten
150g/5oz/1 cup steamed clams or well
drained canned clams,
coarsely chopped
25g/1oz/⅓ cup chopped spring
onions (scallions)
30ml/2 tbsp chopped fresh dill
a few drops of hot pepper sauce
225–350g/8–12oz/1–1½ cups butter or
margarine, melted
salt and ground black pepper

NUTRITION NOTES

Per portion	
Energy	51Kcals/213kJ
Fat	3.4g
Saturated Fat	0.9g
Cholesterol	5mg
Fibre	0

1 Preheat the oven to 200°C/400°F/Gas 6. Stack the sheets of filo pastry and cover with a sheet of clear film (plastic wrap).

2 Combine the soft cheese, egg, clams, spring onions, dill, pepper sauce, and some salt and pepper in a bowl. Mix thoroughly.

3 Lay one sheet of filo pastry on the work surface and brush it lightly and evenly with melted butter. Lay another sheet of filo pastry neatly on top and brush it with butter. Cover with a third sheet of filo pastry and brush with butter.

4 Spoon about one-third of the clam mixture in a line along one side of the stacked filo pastry, about 2.5cm/1in in from the edge.

5 Fold the nearest long filo pastry edge over the clam filling and continue rolling up. Cut the roll across in half and put the two halves on a buttered baking sheet. Brush the rolls with melted butter.

6 Make two more rolls in the same way and put the halves on the baking sheet. Brush them all with melted butter. Bake until golden brown and crisp, for about 20 minutes. Using scissors, cut the rolls across into bite-size pieces. Serve as soon as possible.

Spinach and Cheese Pie

Using low-fat cottage cheese cuts calories with this delicious pie.

1 Preheat the oven to 190°C/375°F/
Gas 5.

2 Stack handfuls of spinach leaves, roll
them loosely, and cut across the
leaves into thin ribbons. Heat the oil in a
large pan. Add the onion and cook until
softened, for about 5 minutes.

3 Add the spinach and oregano and
cook for about 5 minutes over a high
heat until most of the liquid from the
spinach evaporates, stirring frequently.
Remove from the heat and let cool.
Break the eggs into a bowl and beat.
Stir in the cottage cheese and Parmesan
cheese and season generously with
nutmeg, salt and pepper. Stir in the
spinach mixture.

4 Brush a 33 x 23cm/13 x 9in baking
dish with some of the butter or
margarine. Arrange half of the filo sheets
in the bottom of the dish to cover evenly
and extend about 2.5cm/1in up the sides.
Brush with butter.

5 Ladle in the spinach and cheese
filling. Cover with the remaining filo
pastry, tucking under the edge neatly.

6 Brush the top with the remaining
butter. Score the top with diamond
shapes using a sharp knife.

7 Bake for about 30 minutes, or until
the pastry is golden brown. Cut into
squares and serve hot.

Serves 8

1.3g/3lb fresh spinach, coarse
stems removed
30ml/2 tbsp olive oil
1 medium onion, finely chopped
30ml/2 tbsp chopped fresh oregano or
5ml/1 tsp dried oregano
4 eggs
225g/8oz/1 cup creamed low-fat
cottage cheese
90ml/6 tbsp freshly grated
Parmesan cheese
freshly grated nutmeg
50g/2oz/¼ cup butter or
margarine, melted
12 sheets filo pasty, thawed if frozen
salt and ground black pepper

NUTRITION NOTES
Per portion

Energy	299Kcals/1244kJ
Fat	16.4g
Saturated Fat	4.4g
Cholesterol	105mg
Fibre	3.8g

Celeriac Gratin

Although celeriac has a rather unattractive appearance with its hard, knobbly skin, it is a vegetable that has a very delicious sweet and nutty flavour. This is accentuated in this dish by the addition of the sweet yet nutty Emmenthal cheese.

Serves 4

450g/1lb celeriac
juice of ½ lemon
25g/1oz/2 tbsp butter or margarine
1 small onion, finely chopped
30ml/2 tbsp plain (all-purpose) flour
300ml/½ pint/1¼ cups skimmed milk
25g/1oz/¼ cup grated Emmenthal cheese
15ml/1 tbsp capers
salt and cayenne pepper

NUTRITION NOTES

Per portion	
Energy	148Kcals/616kJ
Fat	7.7g
Saturated Fat	2.2g
Cholesterol	8mg
Fibre	4.7g

1 Preheat the oven to 190°C/375°F/ Gas 5. Peel the celeriac and cut into 5mm/¼in slices, immediately plunging them into a pan of cold water acidulated with the lemon juice.

2 Bring the water to the boil and simmer the celeriac for 10–12 minutes until just tender. Drain and arrange the celeriac in a shallow ovenproof dish.

3 Melt the butter in a small pan and fry the onion over a gentle heat until soft but not browned. Stir in the flour, cook for 1 minute, then slowly stir in the milk to make a smooth sauce. Stir in the cheese, capers and seasoning to taste, then pour over the celeriac. Cook in the oven for 15–20 minutes, or until the top is golden brown.

Cook's Tip

For a less strongly flavoured dish, alternate the layers of celeriac with potato. Slice the potato, cook until almost tender, then drain well before assembling the dish.

Baked Leeks with Cheese and Yogurt Topping

Like all vegetables, the fresher leeks are, the better their flavour, and the freshest leeks available should be used for this dish. Small, young leeks are around in late autumn.

1 Preheat the oven to 180°C/350°F/ Gas 4 and butter a shallow ovenproof dish. Trim the leeks, cut a slit from top to bottom and rinse well under cold water.

2 Place the leeks in a pan of water, bring to the boil and simmer gently for 6–8 minutes until just tender. Remove and drain well using a slotted spoon, and arrange in the prepared dish.

3 Beat the eggs with the goat's cheese, yogurt and half the Parmesan cheese, and season well with salt and pepper.

4 Pour the cheese and yogurt mixture over the leeks. Mix the breadcrumbs and remaining Parmesan cheese together and sprinkle over the sauce. Bake in the oven for 30–40 minutes, or until the top is crisp and golden brown.

Serves 4

8 small leeks
2 small (US medium) eggs, beaten
150g/5oz/⅔ cup fresh goat's cheese
85ml/3fl oz/⅓ cup low-fat natural (plain) yogurt
50g/2oz/⅔ cup freshly grated Parmesan cheese
25g/1oz/½ cup fresh white or brown breadcrumbs
salt and ground black pepper

NUTRITION NOTES

Per portion

Energy	259Kcals/1082kJ
Fat	15.5g
Saturated Fat	8.2g
Cholesterol	136mg
Fibre	3.8g

Carrot Soufflés

Use tender young carrots for this light-as-air dish.

Serves 4
450g/1lb carrots
4 eggs, separated
30ml/2 tbsp chopped fresh
coriander (cilantro)
salt and ground black pepper

Cook's Tip
Fresh coriander (cilantro) tastes wonderful and it's well worth growing your own coriander plant in a window box to ensure a regular supply. It is also available freeze-dried in some supermarkets – although less impressive than the fresh variety, it is a better alternative than dried herbs.

NUTRITION NOTES
Per portion

Energy	115Kcals/481kJ
Fat	5.8g
Saturated Fat	1.55g
Cholesterol	192.5mg
Fibre	2.7g

1 Peel the carrots.

2 Cook in salted boiling water for 20 minutes or until tender. Drain, and process until smooth in a food processor.

3 Preheat the oven to 200°C/400°F/ Gas 6. Season the puréed carrots well, and stir in the chopped coriander.

4 Fold the egg yolks into the carrot mixture.

5 In a separate bowl, whisk the egg whites until stiff.

6 Fold the egg whites into the carrot mixture and pour into four greased ramekins. Bake for about 20 minutes or until risen and golden. Serve immediately.

Herb Popovers

Popovers are muffin-size batter puddings with a crisp brown crust and a delicious moist centre.

Makes 12

3 eggs
250ml/8fl oz/1 cup skimmed milk
25g/1oz/2 tbsp butter, melted
75g/3oz/⅔ cup plain (all-purpose) flour
0.75ml/⅛ tsp salt
1 small sprig each mixed fresh herbs,
such as chives, tarragon, dill and parsley

NUTRITION NOTES

Per portion

Energy	75Kcals/316kJ
Fat	3.5g
Saturated Fat	0.8g
Cholesterol	49mg
Fibre	0.3g

1 Preheat the oven to 220°C/425°F/ Gas 7. Grease 12 small ramekins or popover cups.

2 With an electric mixer, beat the eggs until blended. Beat in the milk and melted butter.

3 Sift together the flour and salt, then beat into the egg mixture to combine the ingredients thoroughly.

4 Strip the herb leaves from the stems and chop finely. Mix together and measure out 15ml/1 tbsp. Stir the herbs into the batter.

5 Fill the prepared cups half-full. Bake for 25–30 minutes, or until golden. Do not open the oven door during baking time or the popovers may fall. For drier popovers, pierce each one with a knife after the 30 minutes baking time and bake for 5 minutes more. Serve hot.

Cheese Popovers

Popovers are wonderful when flavoured with a strong cheese such as Parmesan.

1 Preheat the oven to 220°C/425°F/ Gas 7. Grease 12 small ramekins or popover cups.

2 With an electric mixer, beat the eggs until blended. Beat in the milk and melted butter.

3 Sift together the flour, salt and paprika, then beat into the egg mixture. Add the cheese and stir.

4 Fill the prepared cups half-full and bake for 25–30 minutes, or until golden. Do not open the oven door during baking or the popovers may fall. For drier popovers, pierce each one with a knife after the 30 minutes baking time and bake for 5 minutes more. Serve hot.

Variation

To make Yorkshire Pudding Popovers as an accompaniment for roast beef, omit the cheese and use 4–6 tbsp of the pan drippings to replace the butter. Put them into the oven in time to serve warm with the beef.

Makes 12

3 eggs
250ml/8fl oz/1 cup skimmed milk
30ml/2 tbsp butter, melted
75g/3oz/⅔ cup plain (all-purpose) flour
1.5ml/¼ tsp salt
1.5ml/¼ tsp paprika
90ml/6 tbsp freshly grated
Parmesan cheese

NUTRITION NOTES
Per portion
Energy   92Kcals/387kJ
Fat   4.8g
Saturated Fat   1.6g
Cholesterol   52mg
Fibre   0.3g

Pumpkin and Ham Frittata

A frittata is an Italian version of the Spanish tortilla, a substantial omelette made from eggs and vegetables. Although they are sometimes eaten cold, this one tastes better warm or hot, served with crusty bread.

Serves 4

30ml/2 tbsp sunflower oil
1 large onion, chopped
450g/1lb pumpkin, chopped into bitesize pieces
200ml/7fl oz/scant 1 cup chicken stock
115g/4oz/⅔ cup chopped smoked ham
6 eggs
10ml/2 tsp chopped fresh marjoram
salt and ground black pepper

NUTRITION NOTES

Per portion

Energy	231Kcals/962kJ
Fat	15.5g
Saturated Fat	3.5g
Cholesterol	308mg
Fibre	1.8g

1 Preheat the oven to 190°C/375°F/ Gas 5. Oil a large shallow ovenproof dish. Heat the oil in a large frying pan and fry the onion for 3–4 minutes until they are softened.

2 Add the pumpkin and fry over a brisk heat for 3–4 minutes, stirring frequently. Stir in the stock, cover and simmer over a gentle heat for 5–6 minutes until the pumpkin is slightly tender. Add the ham.

3 Pour the mixture into the prepared dish. Beat the eggs with the marjoram and a little seasoning. Pour into the dish and bake for 20–25 minutes until the frittata is firm and lightly golden.

Wholemeal Herb Triangles

Stuffed with cooked chicken and salad, these make a good lunchtime snack and are also an ideal accompaniment to a bowl of steaming soup.

Makes 8

225g/8oz/2 cups plain (all-purpose) wholemeal (whole-wheat) flour
115g/4oz/1 cup strong white bread flour
5ml/1 tsp salt
2.5ml/½ tsp bicarbonate of soda (baking soda)
5ml/1 tsp cream of tartar
2.5ml/½ tsp chilli powder
50g/2oz/¼ cup soft margarine
60ml/4 tbsp chopped mixed fresh herbs
250ml/8fl oz/1 cup skimmed milk
15ml/1 tbsp sesame seeds

NUTRITION NOTES

Per portion

Energy	222Kcals/932kJ
Fat	7.22g
Saturated Fat	1.25g
Cholesterol	1.06mg
Fibre	3.54g

---

1 Preheat the oven to 200°C/400°F/ Gas 6. Lightly flour a baking sheet. Put the wholemeal flour in a mixing bowl. Sift in the remaining dry ingredients, including the chilli powder, then rub in the soft margarine.

3 Carefully cut the dough round into eight wedges, separate them slightly and bake for 15–20 minutes. Transfer to a wire rack to cool. Serve warm or cold.

2 Add the herbs and milk and mix quickly to a soft dough. Turn on to a lightly floured surface. Knead only very briefly or the dough will become tough. Roll out to a 23cm/9in round and place on the prepared baking sheet. Brush lightly with water and sprinkle evenly with the sesame seeds.

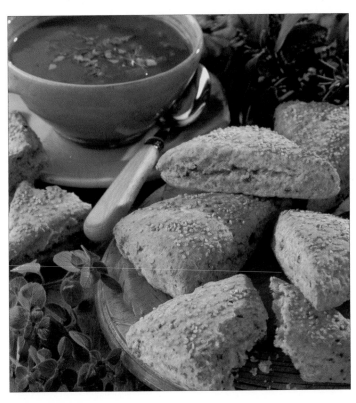

Variation

To make Sun-dried Tomato Triangles, replace the mixed fresh herbs with 30ml/2 tbsp drained chopped sun-dried tomatoes in oil and add 15ml/1 tbsp each mild paprika, chopped fresh parsley and chopped fresh marjoram.

Curry Crackers

These spicy, crisp little nibbles are very low in fat and are ideal for serving with drinks.

Makes 12
50g/2oz/½ cup plain (all-purpose) flour
1.5ml/¼ tsp salt
5ml/1 tsp curry powder
1.5ml/¼ tsp chilli powder
15ml/1 tbsp chopped fresh
coriander (cilantro)
30ml/2 tbsp water

NUTRITION NOTES

Per portion	
Energy	15Kcals/65kJ
Fat	0.11g
Saturated Fat	0.01g
Cholesterol	0
Fibre	0.21g

1 Preheat the oven to 180°C/350°F/ Gas 4. Sift the flour and salt into a mixing bowl, then add the curry powder and chilli powder. Make a well in the centre and add the chopped fresh coriander and water. Gradually incorporate the flour and mix to a firm dough.

2 Turn on to a lightly floured surface, knead until smooth, then leave to rest for 5 minutes.

3 Cut the dough into 12 pieces and knead into small balls. Roll each ball out very thinly to a 10cm/4in round.

4 Arrange the rounds on two ungreased baking sheets, then bake for 15 minutes, turning over once during cooking. Cool on a wire rack.

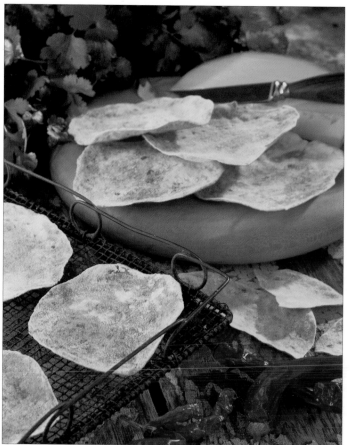

Variation
Omit the curry and chilli powders and add 15ml/1 tbsp caraway, fennel or mustard seeds.

Oatmeal Tartlets with Minted Hummus

Serve these wholesome little tartlets with a crisp salad of cos lettuce.

1 Preheat the oven to 160°C/325°F/ Gas 3. Mix together the oatmeal, bicarbonate of soda and salt in a large bowl. Rub in the butter until the mixture resembles fine crumbs. Stir in the egg yolk and add the milk if the mixture seems too dry.

3 Purée the chick-peas, the juice of one lemon, the fromage blanc and tahini in a food processor until smooth. Spoon into a bowl and season with black pepper and more lemon juice to taste. Stir in the chopped mint. Divide between the tartlet moulds, sprinkle with pumpkin seeds and dust with paprika.

Serves 6

225g/8oz/2 cups medium oatmeal
2.5ml/½ tsp bicarbonate of soda (baking soda)
5ml/1 tsp salt
25g/1oz/2 tbsp butter
1 egg yolk
30ml/2 tbsp skimmed milk
400g/14oz can chick-peas, drained and rinsed
juice of 1–2 lemons
350g/12oz/1½ cups low-fat crème fraîche
60ml/4 tbsp tahini
45ml/3 tbsp chopped fresh mint
25g/1oz/2 tbsp pumpkin seeds
ground black pepper
paprika, for dusting

NUTRITION NOTES

Per portion

Energy	365Kcals/1532kJ
Fat	16.8g
Saturated Fat	2.9g
Cholesterol	35mg
Fibre	5.4g

2 Press into six 9cm/3½in tartlet tins (muffin pans). Bake for 25–30 minutes. Allow to cool.

Ham and Tomato Scones

These scones make an ideal accompaniment for soup. Choose a strongly flavoured ham, trimmed of fat, and chop it fairly finely, so that a little goes a long way. You can use wholemeal flour or a mixture of wholemeal and white flour for extra flavour, if you like.

Serves 12
225g/8oz/2 cups self-raising
(self-rising) flour
5ml/1 tsp dry mustard
5ml/1 tsp paprika, plus extra
for sprinkling
2.5ml/½ tsp salt
25g/1oz/2 tbsp soft margarine
15ml/1 tbsp chopped fresh basil
50g/2oz/1 cup drained sun-dried
tomatoes in oil, chopped
50g/2oz/⅓ cup chopped cooked ham
90–120ml/3–4fl oz/6 tbsp–½ cup
skimmed milk, plus extra for brushing

NUTRITION NOTES
Per portion
Energy   113Kcals/474kJ
Fat   4.23g
Saturated Fat   0.65g
Cholesterol   2.98mg
Fibre   0.65g

 1 Preheat the oven to 200°C/400°F/
Gas 6. Flour a large baking sheet. Sift
the flour, mustard, paprika and salt into a
bowl. Rub in the margarine until the
mixture resembles crumbs.

Cook's Tip
To cut calories and fat, choose dry-packed sun-dried tomatoes and soak them in warm water.

2 Stir in the basil, sun-dried tomatoes and ham, and mix lightly. Pour in enough milk to mix to a soft dough.

3 Turn the dough out on to a lightly floured surface, knead briefly and roll out to a 20 x 15cm/8 x 6in rectangle. Cut into 5cm/2in squares and arrange on the baking sheet.

4 Brush lightly with milk, sprinkle with paprika and bake for about 12–15 minutes. Transfer to a wire rack to cool.

Cheese and Marjoram Scones

A guaranteed success at a hearty tea, these scones can also make a good basis for a light lunch, served with savoury toppings and a crunchy green salad.

1 Gently sift the two kinds of flour into a bowl and add the salt. Cut the butter into small pieces, and rub these into the flour until it resembles fine crumbs.

2 Add the mustard, marjoram and grated cheese, and mix in sufficient milk to make a soft dough. Knead the dough lightly.

3 Preheat the oven to 220°C/425°F/ Gas 7. Roll out the dough on a floured surface to 2cm/¾in thickness and cut it out with a 5cm/2in square cutter. Grease several baking trays with sunflower oil, and place the scones on the trays. Brush the scones with milk and sprinkle the nuts over the top. Bake for 12 minutes. Serve warm.

Serves 18

115g/4oz/1 cup self-raising (self-rising) wholemeal (whole-wheat) flour
115g/4oz/1 cup self-raising (self-rising) flour
pinch of salt
40g/1½oz/3 tbsp butter
1.5ml/¼ tsp dry mustard
10ml/2 tsp dried marjoram
50–75g/2–3oz/½–¾ cup finely grated Cheddar cheese
120ml/4fl oz/½ cup skimmed milk, or as required
5ml/1 tsp sunflower oil
50g/2oz/⅓ cup pecan nuts or walnuts, chopped

NUTRITION NOTES
Per portion
Energy	90Kcals/376kJ
Fat	4.4g
Saturated Fat	0.6g
Cholesterol	1mg
Fibre	0.5g

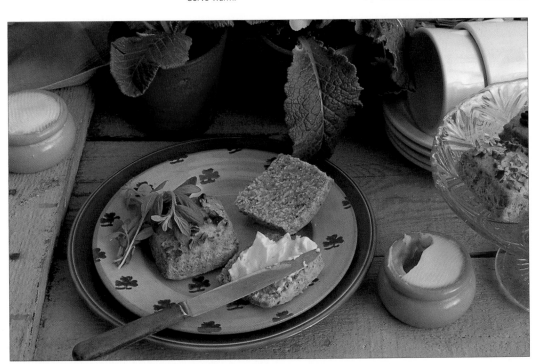

Oatcakes

Try serving these oatcakes with reduced-fat hard cheeses. They are delicious topped with thick honey for breakfast.

Serves 8

175g/6oz/1½ cups medium oatmeal,
plus extra for sprinkling
2.5ml/½ tsp salt
pinch of bicarbonate of soda
(baking soda)
15g/½oz/1 tbsp butter
75ml/5 tbsp water

NUTRITION NOTES

Per portion

Energy	102Kcals/427kJ
Fat	3.43g
Saturated Fat	0.66g
Cholesterol	0.13mg
Fibre	1.49g

1 Preheat the oven to 150°C/300°F/ Gas 2. Mix the oatmeal with the salt and bicarbonate of soda in a bowl.

2 Melt the butter with the water in a small pan. Bring to the boil, then add to the oatmeal mixture and mix to a moist dough.

3 Turn the dough on to a surface sprinkled with oatmeal and knead to a smooth ball. Turn a large baking sheet upside down, grease it, sprinkle it lightly with oatmeal and place the ball of dough on top. Sprinkle the dough with oatmeal, then roll out to a 25cm/10in round.

4 Cut the round into eight sections, ease them apart slightly and bake for about 50–60 minutes until crisp. Leave to cool on the baking sheet, then remove the oatcakes with a metal spatula.

Dill and Potato Cakes

Potato cakes are quite scrumptious and should be more widely made. Try this splendid combination and you are sure to be converted.

1 Preheat the oven to 230°C/450°F/ Gas 8. Sift the flour into a bowl and add the butter, salt and dill. Mix in the mashed potato and enough milk to make a soft, pliable dough.

3 Cut into neat rounds with a 7.5cm/ 3in cutter.

4 Grease a baking sheet, place the cakes on it, and bake for 20–25 minutes until risen and golden.

Serves 10

225g/8oz/2 cups self-raising (self-rising) flour
45ml/3 tbsp butter, softened
pinch of salt
15ml/1 tbsp finely chopped fresh dill
175g/6oz/2 cups mashed potato, freshly made
30–45ml/2–3 tbsp milk, as required

NUTRITION NOTES
Per portion

Energy	121Kcals/510kJ
Fat	4g
Saturated Fat	0.8g
Cholesterol	0
Fibre	0.9g

2 Roll out the dough on a well-floured surface until it is fairly thin.

Chive and Potato Scones

These little scones should be fairly thin, soft in the middle and crisp on the outside. They're extremely quick to make, so serve them for breakfast or lunch.

Serves 20

450g/1lb large potatoes
115g/4oz/1 cup plain (all-purpose) flour, sifted
30ml/2 tbsp olive oil
30ml/2 tbsp chopped chives
salt and ground black pepper
low-fat spread, for topping (optional)

NUTRITION NOTES

Per portion

Energy	50Kcals/211kJ
Fat	1.24g
Saturated Fat	0.17g
Cholesterol	0
Fibre	0.54g

1 Cook the potatoes in a pan of salted boiling water for 20 minutes, then drain thoroughly. Return the potatoes to the clean pan and mash them. Preheat a griddle or heavy frying pan over a low heat.

2 Add the flour, olive oil and chopped chives with a little salt and pepper to the hot mashed potatoes in the pan. Mix to a soft dough.

3 Roll out the dough on a well-floured surface to a thickness of 5mm/¼in and stamp out rounds with a 5cm/2in pastry (cookie) cutter.

4 Cook the scones, in batches, on the hot griddle or frying pan for about 10 minutes until they are golden brown on both sides. Keep the heat low. Top with a little low-fat spread, if you like, and serve immediately.

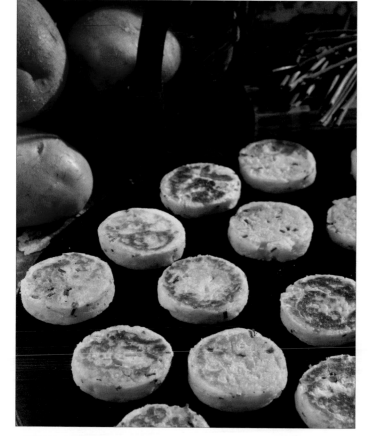

Cheese and Chive Scones

Try serving these savoury scones instead of bread rolls.

Makes 9

115g/4oz/1 cup self-raising (self-rising) white flour
150g/5oz/1¼ cup self-raising (self-rising) wholemeal (whole-wheat) flour
2.5ml/½ tsp salt
75g/3oz/⅓ cup feta cheese
15ml/1 tbsp chopped fresh chives
150ml/¼ pint/⅔ cup skimmed milk, plus extra for glazing
1.5ml/¼ tsp cayenne pepper

NUTRITION NOTES

Per portion

Energy	121Kcals/507kJ
Fat	2.24g
Saturated Fat	1.13g
Cholesterol	0
Fibre	1.92g

1 Preheat the oven to 200°C/400°F/ Gas 6. Sift the flours and salt into a mixing bowl, adding any bran left over from the flour in the sieve.

4 Transfer the scones to a non-stick baking sheet. Brush with skimmed milk, then sprinkle over the cayenne pepper. Bake in the oven for 15 minutes, or until golden.

2 Crumble the feta cheese and rub into the dry ingredients. Stir in the chives, then add the milk and mix to a soft dough.

3 Turn out on to a floured surface and knead lightly until smooth. Roll out to 2cm/¾in thick and stamp out nine scones with a 6cm/2½in biscuit (cookie) cutter.

Desserts

Everyone will adore
these deliciously light
puddings. Serve a fruity
confection to finish a
family meal, or an
elaborate dessert for
a special occasion.

Chestnut and Orange Roulade

This moist cake is ideal to serve as a dessert.

Serves 8
3 eggs, separated
115g/4oz/generous ½ cup caster
(superfine) sugar
225g/8oz/1 cup canned unsweetened
chestnut purée
grated rind and juice of 1 orange
icing (confectioners') sugar, for dusting

For the filling
225g/8oz/1 cup low-fat soft cheese
15ml/1 tbsp clear honey
1 orange

1 Preheat the oven to 180°C/350°/Gas 4. Grease a 30 x 20cm/12 x 8in Swiss roll tin (jelly roll pan) and line with baking parchment. Whisk the egg yolks and sugar in a bowl until thick and creamy.

2 Put the chestnut purée in a separate bowl. Whisk in the orange rind and juice, then whisk the flavoured chestnut purée into the egg mixture.

3 Whisk the egg whites in a grease-free bowl until fairly stiff. Using a metal spoon, stir a generous spoonful of the whites into the chestnut mixture to lighten it, then fold in the rest. Spoon into the prepared tin and bake for 30 minutes until firm. Cool for 5 minutes, then cover with a clean damp dishtowel until completely cold.

4 Meanwhile, make the filling. Put the soft cheese in a bowl with the honey. Finely grate the orange rind and add to the bowl. Peel away all the pith from the orange, cut the fruit into segments, chop roughly and set aside. Add any juice to the cheese mixture, then beat until it is smooth. Mix in the chopped orange.

5 Dust a sheet of baking parchment thickly with icing sugar. Carefully turn the roulade out on to the paper, then peel off the lining paper. Spread the filling over the roulade and roll up like a Swiss (jelly) roll. Transfer to a plate and dust with some more icing sugar.

Cook's Tip

Do not whisk the egg whites too stiffly, or it will be difficult to fold them into the mixture and they will form lumps in the roulade.

NUTRITION NOTES

Per portion

Energy	185Kcals/775kJ
Fat	4.01g
Saturated Fat	1.47g
Cholesterol	76.25mg
Fibre	1.4g

Chocolate, Date and Walnut Pudding

Proper puddings are not totally taboo when you're cutting calories or fat – this one stays within the rules! Serve hot, with yogurt or skimmed-milk custard.

Serves 4

25g/1oz/4 tbsp chopped walnuts
25g/1oz/2 tbsp chopped dates
2 eggs
5ml/1 tsp vanilla essence (extract)
30ml/2 tbsp golden caster (superfine) sugar
45ml/3 tbsp plain (all-purpose) wholemeal (whole-wheat) flour
15ml/1 tbsp cocoa powder (unsweetened)
30ml/2 tbsp skimmed milk

NUTRITION NOTES

Per portion

Energy	169Kcals/708kJ
Fat	8.1g
Saturated Fat	1.7g
Cholesterol	96mg
Fibre	1.8g

1 Preheat the oven to 180°C/350°F/ Gas 4. Grease a 1.2 litre/2 pint/5 cup pudding bowl and place a small circle of baking parchment in the base. Spoon in the walnuts and dates.

2 Separate the eggs and place the yolks in a bowl with the vanilla essence and sugar. Place the bowl over a pan of hot water and whisk until the mixture is thick and pale.

3 Sift the flour and cocoa into the mixture and fold them in with a metal spoon. Stir in the milk, to soften the mixture slightly. Whisk the egg whites until they hold soft peaks and fold them in.

4 Spoon the mixture into the bowl and bake for 40–45 minutes, or until the pudding is well risen and firm to the touch. Run a knife around the pudding to loosen it from the bowl, and then turn it out and serve straight away.

Meringues

This is a basic meringue recipe. These light and airy mouthfuls are excellent
served with low-fat cream.

1 Preheat the oven to 110°C/225°F/
Gas ¼. Line two large baking sheets
with baking parchment.

2 With an electric mixer, beat the egg
whites and salt in a very clean metal
bowl on low speed. When they start to
form soft peaks, add half the sugar and
continue beating until the mixture holds
stiff peaks.

5 Bake for 2 hours. Turn off the oven.
Loosen the meringues, invert, and set
in another place on the sheets to prevent
sticking. Leave in the oven as it cools.
Serve sandwiched with the low-fat
cream, if you like.

Makes 24
4 egg whites
0.75ml/⅛ tsp salt
225g/8oz/generous 1 cup caster
(superfine) sugar
2.5ml/½ tsp vanilla or almond essence
(extract) (optional)
250ml/8fl oz/1 cup low-fat
cream (optional)

NUTRITION NOTES
Per portion

Energy	43Kcals/184kJ
Fat	0
Saturated Fat	0
Cholesterol	0
Fibre	0

3 With a large metal spoon, fold in the
remaining sugar and vanilla or almond
essence, if using.

4 Pipe the meringue mixture or gently
spoon it on to the prepared sheet.

Snowballs

A variation on the basic meringue recipe, these snowballs are made with cornflour.
They make an excellent accompaniment to ice cream.

Makes about 20

2 egg whites
115g/4oz/generous ½ cup caster
(superfine) sugar
15ml/1 tbsp cornflour (cornstarch), sifted
5ml/1 tsp white wine vinegar
1.5ml/¼ tsp vanilla essence (extract)

NUTRITION NOTES

Per portion
Energy	29Kcal/124kJ
Fat	0.01
Saturated Fat	0
Cholesterol	0
Fibre	0

1 Preheat the oven to 150°C/300°F/
Gas 2. Line two baking sheets with
baking parchment. Whisk the egg whites
in a large grease-free bowl until very stiff,
using an electric whisk.

2 Add the sugar, whisking until the
meringue is very stiff. Whisk in the
cornflour, vinegar and vanilla essence.

3 Drop teaspoonfuls of the mixture on
to the baking sheets, shaping them
into mounds, and bake for 30 minutes
until crisp.

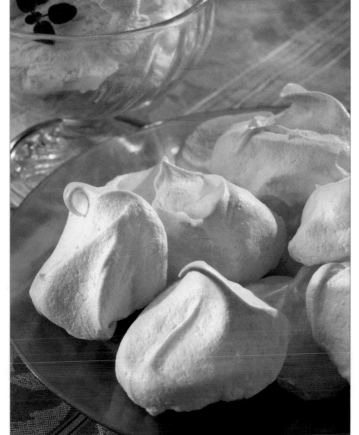

4 Remove from the oven and leave
to cool on the baking sheet. When
the snowballs are cold, remove them
from the paper with a palette knife
(metal spatula).

Muscovado Meringues

These light brown meringues are extremely low in fat and are delicious served on their own or sandwiched together with a fresh fruit soft cheese filling.

1 Preheat the oven to 160°C/325°F/ Gas 3. Line two baking sheets with baking parchment. Press the sugar through a metal sieve into a bowl.

4 Sprinkle the meringues with the walnuts. Bake for 30 minutes. Cool for 5 minutes on the baking sheets, then leave on a wire rack.

Makes about 20

115g/4oz/½ cup light muscovado (brown) sugar
2 egg whites
5ml/1 tsp finely chopped walnuts

NUTRITION NOTES

Per portion	
Energy	197Kcals/826kJ
Fat	6.8g
Saturated Fat	1.4g
Cholesterol	25mg
Fibre	0.7g

2 Whisk the egg whites in a clean, dry bowl, until very stiff and dry, then whisk in the sugar, about 15ml/1 tbsp at a time, until the meringue is very thick and glossy.

3 Spoon small mounds of the mixture on to the prepared baking sheets.

Raspberry Vacherin

Meringue rounds filled with orange-flavoured fromage frais and fresh raspberries makes a perfect dinner party dessert.

Serves 6
3 egg whites
175g/6oz/scant 1 cup caster (superfine) sugar
5ml/1 tsp chopped almonds
icing (confectioners') sugar, for dusting
raspberry leaves, to decorate (optional)

For the filling
175g/6oz/¾ cup low-fat soft cheese
15–30ml/1–2 tbsp clear honey
15ml/1 tbsp Cointreau
120ml/4 fl oz/½ cup low-fat fromage frais or low-fat crème fraîche
225g/8oz/1¼ cup raspberries

Cook's Tip
When making the meringue, whisk the egg whites until they are so stiff that you can turn the bowl upside down without them falling out.

NUTRITION NOTES
Per portion
Energy	248Kcals/1041kJ
Fat	2.22g
Saturated Fat	0.82g
Cholesterol	4mg
Fibre	1.06g

1 Preheat the oven to 140°C/275°F/ Gas 1. Draw a 20cm/8in circle on two pieces of baking parchment. Turn the paper over so the marking is on the underside and use it to line two heavy baking sheets.

2 Whisk the egg whites in a grease-free bowl until very stiff, then gradually whisk in the caster sugar to make a stiff meringue mixture.

3 Spoon the mixture on to the circles on the prepared baking sheets, spreading the meringue evenly to the edges. Sprinkle one meringue round with the chopped almonds.

4 Bake for 1½–2 hours, then carefully lift the meringue rounds off the baking sheets, peel away the paper and cool on a wire rack.

5 To make the filling, cream the soft cheese with the honey and liqueur in a bowl. Fold in the fromage frais and raspberries, reserving three of the best for decoration.

6 Place the plain meringue round on a board, spread with the filling and top with the nut-covered round. Dust with icing sugar, transfer to a serving plate and decorate with the reserved raspberries, and a sprig of raspberry leaves, if you like.

Toasted Oat Meringues

The oats add an unusual flavour and texture to this interesting dessert.

Makes 12

115g/4oz/1 cup jumbo oats
2 egg whites
0.75ml/⅛ tsp salt
7.5ml/1½ tsp cornflour (cornstarch)
175g/6oz/scant 1 cup caster
(superfine) sugar

NUTRITION NOTES

Per portion

Energy	98Kcals/416kJ
Fat	0.8g
Saturated Fat	0.2g
Cholesterol	0
Fibre	0.6g

1 Preheat the oven to 140°C/275°F/ Gas 1. Spread the oats on a baking sheet and toast in the oven until golden, for about 10 minutes. Remove the oats and lower the heat to 120°C/250°F/ Gas ½. Line a baking sheet with baking parchment.

Variation

Add 2.5ml/½ tsp ground cinnamon with the oats, and fold in gently.

2 With an electric mixer, beat the egg whites and salt until they start to form soft peaks.

3 Sift over the cornflour and continue beating until the whites hold stiff peaks. Add half the sugar and whisk until glossy.

4 Add the remaining sugar and fold in, then fold in the toasted oats.

5 Gently spoon mounds of the mixture on to the prepared sheet and bake for 2 hours.

6 When done, turn off the oven. Lift the meringues from the tray, turn over, and set in another place on the sheet to prevent sticking. Leave in the oven as it cools down.

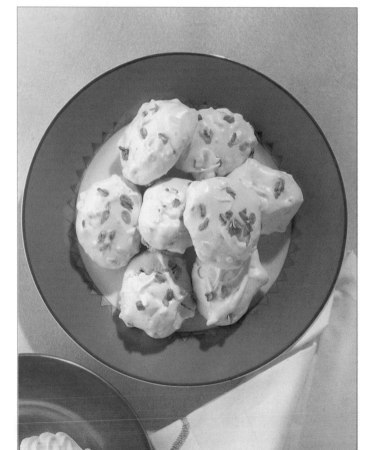

Feather-light Peach Pudding

On chilly days, try this hot fruit pudding with its tantalizing sponge topping.

1 Preheat the oven to 180°C/350°F/ Gas 4. Drain the peaches and put into a 1 litre/1¾ pint/4 cup pie dish with 30ml/2 tbsp of the juice.

4 Lightly dust the top with icing sugar before serving hot with the custard.

2 Put all the remaining ingredients, except the icing sugar, into a mixing bowl. Beat for 3–4 minutes, until thoroughly combined.

3 Spoon the sponge mixture over the peaches and level the top evenly. Cook in the oven for 35–40 minutes, or until springy to the touch.

Cook's Tip

For a simple sauce, blend 5ml/1 tsp arrowroot with 15ml/1 tbsp peach juice in a small pan. Stir in the remaining peach juice from the can and bring to the boil. Simmer for 1 minute until thickened and clear.

Serves 4

400g/14oz/3 cups canned peach slices in natural juice
50g/2oz/4 tbsp low-fat spread
40g/1½oz/3 tbsp soft light brown sugar
1 egg, beaten
50g/2oz/½ cup plain (all-purpose) wholemeal (whole-wheat) flour
50g/2oz/½ cup plain (all-purpose) white flour
5ml/1 tsp baking powder
2.5ml/½ tsp ground cinnamon
60ml/4 tbsp skimmed milk
2.5ml/½ tsp vanilla essence (extract)
10ml/2 tsp icing (confectioners') sugar
low-fat ready-to-serve custard, to serve

NUTRITION NOTES
Per portion

Energy	255Kcals/1071kJ
Fat	6.78g
Saturated Fat	1.57g
Cholesterol	35mg
Fibre	2.65g

Strawberry Gâteau

It's hard to believe that this delicious gâteau is low in fat, but it's true, so enjoy!

Serves 6
2 eggs
75g/3oz/scant ½ cup caster
(superfine) sugar
grated rind of ½ orange
50g/2oz/½ cup plain (all-purpose) flour
icing (confectioners') sugar, for dusting
strawberry leaves, to decorate (optional)

For the filling
275g/10oz/1¼ cups low-fat soft cheese
grated rind of ½ orange
30ml/2 tbsp caster (superfine) sugar
60ml/4 tbsp low-fat fromage frais or
low-fat crème fraîche
225g/8oz/2 cups strawberries, halved
25g/1oz/2 tbsp chopped
almonds, toasted

Cook's Tip
Use other soft fruits in season,
such as currants, raspberries,
blackberries or blueberries, or
try a mixture of different berries.

NUTRITION NOTES
Per portion
Energy	213Kcals/893kJ
Fat	6.08g
Saturated Fat	1.84g
Cholesterol	70.22mg
Fibre	1.02g

1 Preheat the oven to 190°C/375°F/ Gas 5. Grease a 30 x 20cm/12 x 8in Swiss roll tin (jelly roll pan) and line with baking parchment.

2 In a bowl, whisk the eggs, sugar and orange rind together with a hand-held electric whisk until thick and mousse-like (when the whisk is lifted, a trail should remain on the surface of the mixture for at least 15 seconds).

3 Fold in the flour with a metal spoon, being careful not to knock out any air. Turn into the prepared tin. Bake for 15–20 minutes, or until the cake springs back when lightly pressed. Turn the cake on to a wire rack, remove the lining paper and leave to cool.

4 Meanwhile make the filling. In a bowl, mix the soft cheese with the orange rind, sugar and fromage frais until smooth. Divide between two bowls. Chop half the strawberry halves and add to one bowl of filling.

5 Cut the sponge widthways into three equal pieces and sandwich them together with the strawberry filling. Spread two-thirds of the plain filling over the sides of the cake and press on the toasted almonds.

6 Spread the rest of the filling over the top of the cake and decorate with strawberry halves, and strawberry leaves if you like. Dust with icing sugar and transfer to a serving plate.

Baked Blackberry Cheesecake

This light, low-fat cheesecake is best made with wild blackberries, if they're available, but cultivated ones will do; or substitute other soft fruit, such as loganberries, raspberries or blueberries.

Serves 5

175g/6oz/¾ cup low-fat cottage cheese
150g/5oz/⅔ cup low-fat natural
(plain) yogurt
15ml/1 tbsp plain (all-purpose)
wholemeal (whole-wheat) flour
25g/1oz/2 tbsp golden caster
(superfine) sugar
1 egg
1 egg white
finely grated rind and juice of ½ lemon
200g/7oz/1¾ cups fresh or frozen and
thawed blackberries

Cook's Tip

If you prefer to use canned blackberries, choose those canned in natural juice and drain the fruit well before adding it to the cheesecake mixture. The juice can be served with the cheesecake, but this will increase the total calories.

NUTRITION NOTES

Per portion

Energy	103Kcals/437kJ
Fat	2g
Saturated Fat	0.8g
Cholesterol	41mg
Fibre	1.6g

1 Preheat the oven to 180°C/350°F/ Gas 4. Lightly grease and base-line an 18cm/7in sandwich tin (pan).

2 Place the cottage cheese in a food processor and process until smooth. Alternatively, rub it though a sieve to obtain a smooth mixture.

3 Add the yogurt, flour, sugar, egg and egg white and mix. Add the lemon rind, juice and blackberries, reserving a few for decoration.

4 Tip the mixture into the prepared tin and bake for 30–35 minutes, or until it is just set. Turn off the oven and leave for a further 30 minutes.

5 Run a knife around the edge of the cheesecake, then turn it out. Remove the lining paper and place on a warm serving plate.

6 Decorate with the reserved blackberries and serve warm.

Cherry Clafoutis

When fresh cherries are in season, this makes a deliciously simple dessert for any occasion.
Serve warm with a little low-fat fromage frais or crème fraîche.

Serves 6

675g/1½lb/4 cups fresh cherries
50g/2oz/½ cup plain (all-purpose) flour
pinch of salt
4 eggs, plus 2 egg yolks
115g/4oz/generous ½ cup caster
(superfine) sugar
600ml/1 pint/2½ cups skimmed milk
50g/2oz/¼ cup melted butter
caster (superfine) sugar, for dusting

NUTRITION NOTES

Per portion

Energy	312Kcals/1308kJ
Fat	12.6g
Saturated Fat	2.9g
Cholesterol	19mg
Fibre	1g

1 Preheat the oven to 190°C/375°F/ Gas 5. Lightly butter the base and sides of a shallow ovenproof dish. Stone the cherries and place in the dish.

2 Sift the flour and salt into a bowl. Add the eggs, egg yolks, sugar and a little of the milk and whisk to a smooth batter.

3 Gradually whisk in the rest of the milk and the butter, then strain the batter over the cherries. Bake for 40–50 minutes until golden and just set. Serve warm, dusted with caster sugar, if you like.

Cook's Tip

Use two 425g/15oz cans stoned black cherries, thoroughly drained, if fresh cherries are not available. For a special dessert, add 45ml/3 tbsp kirsch to the batter.

Filo Fruit Baskets

These little baskets are an easy dinner party dessert.

1 Preheat the oven to 180°C/350°F/Gas 4. Grease six cups of a muffin tin (pan).

2 Stack the filo sheets and cut with a sharp knife or scissors into 24 x 12cm/4½ in squares.

3 Lay four squares of pastry in each of the six muffin cups. Press the pastry firmly into the cups, rotating slightly to make star-shaped baskets.

4 Brush the pastry baskets lightly with butter or margarine. Bake for 5–7 minutes, or until the pastry is crisp and golden. Cool on a wire rack.

5 In a bowl, lightly whip the cream until soft peaks form. Gently fold the strawberry preserves and orange liqueur into the cream.

6 Just before serving, spoon a little of the cream mixture into each pastry basket. Top with the fruit. Sprinkle with icing sugar and decorate each basket with a small sprig of mint.

Serves 6

4 large or 8 small sheets filo pastry, thawed if frozen
65g/2½oz/5 tbsp butter or margarine, melted
250ml/8fl oz/1 cup whipping cream
75g/3oz/¼ cup strawberry preserve
15ml/1 tbsp Cointreau or other orange liqueur
175g/6oz/1 cup seedless red grapes, halved
175g/6oz/1 cup seedless green grapes, halved
175g/6oz fresh pineapple, cubed
175g/6oz/1 cup raspberries
30ml/2 tbsp icing (confectioners') sugar
6 small sprigs of fresh mint, to decorate

NUTRITION NOTES
Per portion

Energy	255Kcals/1063kJ
Fat	11g
Saturated Fat	2.2g
Cholesterol	1mg
Fibre	0.9g

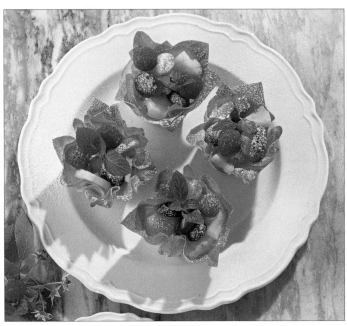

Blueberry and Orange Crêpe Baskets

Impress your guests with these pretty, fruit-filled crêpes. When blueberries are out of season, replace them with other soft fruit, such as raspberries.

Serves 6

For the pancakes
150g/5oz/1¼ cups plain
(all-purpose) flour
pinch of salt
2 egg whites
200ml/7fl oz/scant 1 cup skimmed milk
150ml/¼ pint/⅔ cup orange juice

For the filling
4 medium-size oranges
225g/8oz/2 cups blueberries

1 Preheat the oven to 200°C/400°F/ Gas 6. To make the pancakes, sift the flour and salt into a bowl. Make a well in the centre of the flour and add the egg whites, milk and orange juice. Whisk hard, until all the liquid has been incorporated and the batter is smooth and bubbly.

4 Place six small ovenproof bowls or moulds on a baking sheet and arrange the pancakes over these. Bake the pancakes in the oven for about 10 minutes, until they are crisp and set into the shape of the moulds. Carefully lift the "baskets" off the moulds.

5 For the filling, pare a thin piece of orange rind from one orange and cut it into fine strips. Blanch the strips in boiling water for 30 seconds, rinse in cold water and set aside. Cut all the peel and white pith from all the oranges.

2 Lightly grease a heavy or non-stick pancake pan and heat until it is very hot. Pour in just enough batter to cover the base of the pan, swirling it to cover the pan evenly.

Cook's Tip
Don't fill the pancake baskets until you're ready to serve them, because they will absorb the fruit juice and begin to soften.

NUTRITION NOTES
Per portion

Energy	159Kcals/673kJ
Fat	0.5g
Saturated Fat	0.1g
Cholesterol	1mg
Fibre	3.3g

3 Cook until the pancake has set and is golden, and then turn it to cook the other side. Remove the pancake to a sheet of kitchen paper, and then cook the remaining batter, to make 6–8 pancakes.

6 Divide the oranges into segments, catching the juice, combine with the blueberries and warm them gently. Spoon the fruit into the baskets and scatter the shreds of rind over the top. Serve with yogurt or light crème fraîche.

Filo and Apricot Purses

Filo pastry is very easy to use and is low in fat. Keep a packet in the freezer ready for rustling up a speedy tea-time treat.

Makes 12

115g/4oz/½ cup ready-to-eat
dried apricots
45ml/3 tbsp apricot compote
or conserve
3 amaretti, crushed
3 sheets filo pastry, thawed if frozen
20ml/4 tsp soft margarine, melted
icing (confectioners') sugar, for dusting

NUTRITION NOTES

Per portion
Energy	58Kcals/245kJ
Fat	1.85g
Saturated Fat	0.4g
Cholesterol	0.12mg
Fibre	0.74g

1 Preheat the oven to 180°C/350°F/ Gas 4. Grease two baking sheets. Chop the apricots, put them in a bowl and stir in the apricot compote. Add the crushed amaretti and mix well.

2 Cut the filo pastry into 24 13cm/5in squares, pile the squares on top of each other and cover with a clean dishtowel to prevent the pastry from drying out and becoming brittle.

3 Lay one pastry square on a flat surface, brush lightly with melted margarine and lay another square diagonally on top. Brush the top square with melted margarine. Spoon a small mound of apricot mixture in the centre of the pastry, bring up the edges and pinch together in a money-bag shape. Repeat with the remaining filo squares and filling to make 12 purses in all.

4 Arrange the purses on the prepared baking sheets and bake for 5–8 minutes until golden brown. Transfer to a wire rack and dust lightly with icing sugar. Serve warm.

Filo Scrunchies

Quick and easy to make, these pastries are ideal to serve at tea time. Eat them warm or they will lose their crispness.

1 Preheat the oven to 190°C/375°F/ Gas 5. Halve the apricots or plums, remove the stones (pits) and slice the fruit. Cut the filo pastry into twelve 18cm/7in squares. Pile the squares on top of each other and cover with a clean dishtowel to prevent the pastry from drying out.

4 Place the scrunchies on a baking sheet. Bake for 8–10 minutes until golden brown, then loosen the scrunchies from the baking sheet with a metal spatula and transfer to a wire rack. Dust with icing sugar and serve at once.

Makes 6

5 apricots or plums
4 sheets filo pastry, thawed if frozen
20ml/4 tsp soft margarine, melted
50g/2oz/¼ cup demerara (raw) sugar
30ml/2 tbsp flaked (sliced) almonds
icing (confectioners') sugar, for dusting

NUTRITION NOTES

Per portion

Energy	132Kcals/555kJ
Fat	4.19g
Saturated Fat	0.63g
Cholesterol	0
Fibre	0.67g

2 Remove one square of filo and brush it with melted margarine. Lay a second filo square on top, then, using your fingers, mould the pastry into folds. Make five more scrunchies in the same way, working quickly so that the pastry does not dry out.

3 Arrange a few slices of fruit in the folds of each scrunchie, then sprinkle generously with the demerara sugar and flaked almonds.

Plum Filo Pockets

These attractive party parcels are high in fibre as well as being a tasty treat.

Serves 4

115g/4oz/½ cup skimmed-
milk soft cheese
15ml/1 tbsp light muscovado
(brown) sugar
2.5ml/½ tsp ground cloves
8 large, firm plums, halved and stoned
8 sheets filo pastry, thawed if frozen
sunflower oil, for brushing
icing (confectioners') sugar, to sprinkle

NUTRITION NOTES

Per portion

Energy	188Kcals/790kJ
Fat	1.87g
Saturated Fat	0.27g
Cholesterol	0.29mg
Fibre	2.55g

1 Preheat the oven to 220°C/425°F/ Gas 7. Mix together the cheese, sugar and cloves.

2 Sandwich the plum halves back together with a spoonful of the cheese mixture in each plum.

3 Spread out the pastry and cut into 16 pieces, about 23cm/9in square. Brush one lightly with oil and place a second at a diagonal on top. Repeat with the remaining squares.

4 Place a plum on each pastry square, and gather the corners together. Place on a baking sheet. Bake for 15–18 minutes, until golden, then dust with icing sugar.

Apple Couscous Pudding

This unusual mixture makes a delicious family pudding with a rich, fruity flavour, but virtually no fat.

Serves 4

600ml/1 pint/2½ cups apple juice
115g/4oz/⅔ cup couscous
40g/1½oz/3 tbsp sultanas
(golden raisins)
2.5ml/½ tsp mixed (apple pie) spice
1 large cooking apple
30ml/2 tbsp demerara (raw) sugar
low-fat natural (plain) yogurt, to serve

NUTRITION NOTES

Per portion	
Energy	194Kcals/815kJ
Fat	0.58g
Saturated Fat	0.09g
Cholesterol	0
Fibre	0.75g

1 Preheat the oven to 200°C/400°F/ Gas 6. Place the apple juice, couscous, sultanas and spice in a pan and bring to the boil, stirring. Cover and simmer for 10–12 minutes, until all the free liquid is absorbed.

3 Arrange the remaining apple slices overlapping on top and sprinkle with demerara sugar. Bake for 25–30 minutes, or until golden brown. Serve hot, with low-fat yogurt.

2 Peel, core and slice the apple. Spoon half the couscous mixture into a 1.2 litre/2 pint/5 cup ovenproof dish and top with half the apple slices. Top with the remaining couscous.

Filo Chiffon Pie

Filo pastry is low in fat and very easy to use. Here is an interesting and delicious alternative to rhubarb crumbles and pies that are more traditional.

Serves 3

500g/1¼lb pink rhubarb
5ml/1 tsp mixed (apple pie) spice
finely grated rind and juice of 1 orange
15ml/1 tsp granulated sweetener
15g/½oz/1 tbsp butter
3 sheets filo pastry, thawed if frozen

1 Preheat the oven to 200°C/400°F/ Gas 6. Trim the leaves and ends from the rhubarb sticks and chop them in 2.5cm/1in pieces. Place them in a bowl.

3 Melt the butter and brush it over the pastry. Lift the pastry on to the pie dish, butter-side up, and crumple it up to form a chiffon effect, covering the pie completely.

2 Add the mixed spice, orange rind and juice and sweetener and toss well to coat evenly. Tip the rhubarb into a 1 litre/1¾ pint/4 cup pie dish.

4 Place the dish on a baking sheet and bake it for 20 minutes, until golden brown. Reduce the heat to 180°C/350°F/ Gas 4 and bake for a further 10–15 minutes, until the rhubarb is tender. Serve warm.

Variation

Other fruit such as apples, pears or peaches can be used in this pie – try it with whatever is in season.

NUTRITION NOTES

Per portion

Energy	158Kcals/660kJ
Fat	5.3g
Saturated Fat	1g
Cholesterol	0
Fibre	2.4g

Mango and Amaretti Strudel

Fresh mango and crushed amaretti wrapped in wafer-thin filo pastry make a special treat that is equally delicious made with apricots or plums.

Serves 4

1 large mango
grated rind of 1 lemon
2 amaretti
25g/1oz/2 tbsp demerara (raw) sugar
60ml/4 tbsp wholemeal
(whole-wheat) breadcrumbs
2 sheets filo pastry, each 48 x 28cm/
19 x 11in, thawed if frozen
20g/¾oz/4 tsp soft margarine, melted
15ml/1 tbsp chopped almonds
icing (confectioners') sugar, for dusting

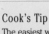

Cook's Tip

The easiest way to prepare a mango is to cut horizontally through the fruit, keeping the knife blade close to the stone. Repeat on the other side of the stone and peel off the skin. Remove the remaining skin and flesh from around the stone.

NUTRITION NOTES

Per portion

Energy	239Kcals/1006kJ
Fat	8.45g
Saturated Fat	4.43g
Cholesterol	17.25mg
Fibre	3.3g

1 Preheat the oven to 190°C/375°F/ Gas 5. Lightly grease a large baking sheet. Halve, stone and peel the mango. Cut the flesh into cubes, then place them in a bowl, and sprinkle with grated lemon rind.

2 Crush the amaretti and mix them with the demerara sugar and the wholemeal breadcrumbs.

3 Lay one sheet of filo on a flat surface and brush with a quarter of the melted margarine. Top with the second sheet, brush with one-third of the remaining margarine, then fold both sheets over, if necessary, to make a rectangle measuring 28 x 23cm/11 x 9in. Brush with half the remaining margarine.

4 Sprinkle the filo with the amaretti mixture, leaving a 5cm/2in border on each long side. Arrange the mango cubes over the top.

5 Roll up the filo from one of the long sides like a Swiss roll (jelly roll). Lift the strudel on to the baking sheet with the join underneath. Brush with the remaining melted margarine and sprinkle with the chopped almonds.

6 Bake for 20–25 minutes until golden brown, then transfer to a board. Dust with the icing sugar, slice diagonally and serve warm.

Chunky Apple Bake

This filling, economical family pudding is a good way to use up slightly stale bread – any type of bread will do, but wholemeal is richest in fibre.

Serves 4

450g/1lb cooking apples
75g/3oz wholemeal (whole-wheat) bread, without crusts
115g/4oz/½ cup low-fat cottage cheese
45ml/3 tbsp light muscovado (brown) sugar
200ml/7fl oz/scant 1 cup semi-skimmed milk
5ml/1 tsp demerara (raw) sugar

1 Preheat the oven to 220°C/425°F/ Gas 7. Peel the apples, cut them into quarters and remove the cores.

4 Toss together the apples, bread, cottage cheese and muscovado sugar in a bowl.

2 Roughly chop the apples into even-size pieces, about 1cm/½in across.

5 Stir in the milk and then tip the mixture into a wide ovenproof dish. Sprinkle with the demerara sugar.

Cook's Tip
You may need to adjust the amount of milk used, depending on the dryness of the bread; the more stale the bread, the more milk it will absorb.

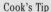

NUTRITION NOTES
Per portion

Energy	168Kcals/707kJ
Fat	1g
Saturated Fat	0.4g
Cholesterol	2mg
Fibre	2.9g

3 Cut the bread into 1cm/½in dice.

6 Bake for 30–35 minutes, or until golden brown and bubbling. Serve hot.

Baked Apple in Honey and Lemon

A classic mix of flavours in a healthy, traditional family pudding. Serve warm, with skimmed-milk custard.

Serves 4
4 medium-size cooking apples
15ml/1 tbsp clear honey
grated rind and juice of 1 lemon
15ml/1 tbsp low-fat spread

NUTRITION NOTES
Per portion

Energy	651Kcals/2703kJ
Fat	1.7g
Saturated Fat	0.4g
Cholesterol	0
Fibre	1.7g

1 Preheat the oven to 180°C/350°F/ Gas 4. Remove the cores from the apples, leaving them whole.

2 With a cannelle or sharp knife, cut lines through the apple skin at intervals and place in an ovenproof dish.

3 Mix together the honey, lemon rind, juice and low-fat spread.

4 Spoon the mixture into the apples and cover the dish with foil or a lid. Bake for 40–45 minutes, or until the apples are tender. Serve with skimmed-milk custard.

Strawberry and Apple Crumble

A high fibre, healthier version of the classic apple crumble. Raspberries can be used instead of strawberries, either fresh or frozen. Serve warm, with skimmed-milk custard.

Serves 4

450g/1lb cooking apples
150g/5oz/1¼ cups strawberries, hulled
30ml/2 tbsp granulated sweetener
2.5ml/½ tsp ground cinnamon
30ml/2 tbsp orange juice

For the crumble

45ml/3 tbsp plain (all-purpose)
wholemeal (whole-wheat) flour
50g/2oz/⅔ cups rolled oats
25g/1oz/2 tbsp low-fat spread

NUTRITION NOTES

Per portion

Energy	182Kcals/769kJ
Fat	4g
Saturated Fat	0.9g
Cholesterol	0
Fibre	3.5g

1 Preheat the oven to 180°C/350°F/ Gas 4. Peel, core and slice the apples. Halve the strawberries.

4 Sprinkle the crumble evenly over the fruit. Bake for 40–45 minutes (20–25 minutes for individual dishes), until golden brown and bubbling. Serve warm, with low-fat custard or yogurt.

2 Toss together the apples, strawberries, sweetener, cinnamon and orange juice. Tip into a 1.2 litre/2 pint/5 cup ovenproof dish, or four individual dishes.

3 Combine the flour and oats in a bowl and mix in the low-fat spread with a fork.

Mixed Berry Tart

The orange-flavoured pastry in this tart is delicious with the fresh fruits of summer.
Serve this with some extra shreds of orange rind scattered on top.

Serves 8

For the pastry
225g/8oz/2 cups plain
(all-purpose) flour
115g/4oz/½ cup unsalted (sweet) butter
finely grated rind of 1 orange, plus
extra to decorate

For the filling
300ml/½ pint/1¼ cups crème fraîche
finely grated rind of 1 lemon
10ml/2 tsp icing (confectioners') sugar
675g/1½lb/6 cups mixed
summer berries

1 To make the pastry, put the flour and butter in a large bowl. Using your fingertips, rub in the butter until the mixture resembles crumbs.

2 Add the orange rind and enough cold water to make a soft dough.

3 Roll into a ball and chill for at least 20 minutes. Roll out the pastry on a lightly floured surface.

4 Line a 23cm/9in loose-based flan tin (tart pan) with the pastry. Chill for 30 minutes. Preheat the oven to 200°C/400°F/Gas 6 and place a baking sheet in the oven to heat up. Weight the pastry base with baking parchment and baking beans and bake blind on the baking sheet for 15 minutes. Remove the paper and beans and bake the pastry for about 10 minutes, until it is golden. Allow to cool.

5 To make the filling, whisk the crème fraîche, lemon rind and sugar together and pour into the pastry case (pie crust). Top with fruit, sprinkle with orange rind and serve sliced.

NUTRITION NOTES
Per portion

Energy	293Kcals/1223kJ
Fat	17.9g
Saturated Fat	5.9g
Cholesterol	40mg
Fibre	2.4g

Crunchy Gooseberry Crumble

Gooseberries are perfect for traditional family puddings like this one. When they are out of season, other fruits such as apples, plums or rhubarb could be used instead.

Serves 4
500g/1¼lb/5 cups gooseberries
50g/2oz/¼ cup caster (superfine) sugar
75g/3oz/scant 1 cup rolled oats
75g/3oz/⅔ cup plain (all-purpose)
wholemeal (whole-wheat) flour
60ml/4 tbsp sunflower oil
50g/2oz/¼ cup demerara (raw) sugar
30ml/2 tbsp chopped walnuts
low-fat yogurt or custard, to serve

NUTRITION NOTES
Per portion

Energy	422Kcals/1770kJ
Fat	18.5g
Saturated Fat	2.32g
Cholesterol	0
Fibre	5.12g

1 Preheat the oven to 200°C/400°F/ Gas 6. Place the gooseberries in a pan with the caster sugar. Cover the pan and cook over a low heat for 10 minutes, until the gooseberries are just tender. Tip into an ovenproof dish.

2 To make the crumble, place the oats, flour and oil in a bowl, and stir with a fork until evenly mixed.

3 Stir in the demerara sugar and walnuts, then spread evenly over the gooseberries. Bake for 25–30 minutes, or until golden and bubbling. Serve hot with low-fat yogurt, or custard made with skimmed milk.

Cook's Tip
The best cooking gooseberries are the early small, firm green ones.

Ginger Upside Down Pudding

A traditional pudding goes down well on a cold winter's day. This one is quite quick to make and looks very impressive.

1 Preheat the oven to 180°C/350°F/ Gas 4. For the topping, brush the base and sides of a 23cm/9in round spring-form cake tin (pan) with oil. Sprinkle the sugar over the base.

2 Arrange the peaches cut-side down in the tin with a walnut half in each.

3 For the base, sift together the flour, bicarbonate of soda, ginger and cinnamon, then stir in the sugar. Beat together the egg, milk and oil, then mix into the dry ingredients until smooth.

4 Pour the mixture evenly over the peaches and bake for 35–40 minutes, until firm to the touch. Turn out on to a serving plate. Serve hot with low-fat yogurt or custard.

Serves 4–6
sunflower oil, for brushing
15ml/1 tbsp soft brown sugar
4 medium peaches, halved and stoned
8 walnut halves

For the base
115g/4oz/½ cup plain (all-purpose) wholemeal (whole-wheat) flour
2.5ml/½ tsp bicarbonate of soda (baking soda)
7.5ml/1½ tsp ground ginger
5ml/1 tsp ground cinnamon
115g/4oz/½ cup dark muscovado (molasses) sugar
1 egg
120ml/4fl oz/½ cup skimmed milk
50ml/2fl oz/¼ cup sunflower oil

NUTRITION NOTES
Per portion
Energy	432Kcals/1812kJ
Fat	16.54g
Saturated Fat	2.27g
Cholesterol	48.72mg
Fibre	4.79g

Latticed Peaches

An elegant dessert; it certainly doesn't look low in fat, but it really is. Use canned peach halves when fresh peaches are out of season, or if you're short of time.

Serves 6

For the pastry
115g/4oz/1 cup plain (all-purpose) flour
40g/1½oz/3 tbsp butter or
sunflower margarine
45ml/3 tbsp low-fat natural
(plain) yogurt
30ml/2 tbsp orange juice
skimmed milk, for glaze

For the filling
3 ripe peaches or nectarines
45ml/3 tbsp ground almonds
30ml/2 tbsp low-fat natural
(plain) yogurt
finely grated rind of 1 small orange
1.5ml/¼ tsp natural almond
essence (extract)

For the sauce
1 ripe peach or nectarine
45ml/3 tbsp orange juice

1 For the pastry, sift the flour into a bowl and, using your fingertips, rub in the butter or margarine evenly. Stir in the yogurt and orange juice to bind the mixture into a firm dough.

4 Roll out the remaining pastry thinly and cut into thin strips. Arrange the strips over the peaches to form a lattice, brushing with milk to secure firmly. Trim off the ends neatly.

2 Roll out about half the pastry thinly and use a biscuit cutter to stamp out rounds about 7.5cm/3in in diameter, slightly larger than the circumference of the peaches. Place on a lightly greased baking sheet.

5 Chill in the fridge for 30 minutes. Preheat the oven to 200°C/400°F/ Gas 6. Brush with milk and bake for 15–18 minutes, until golden brown.

Cook's Tip
This dessert is best eaten fairly fresh from the oven, as the pastry can toughen slightly if left to stand. So assemble the peaches in their pastry on a baking sheet, chill in the refrigerator, and bake just before serving.

NUTRITION NOTES
Per portion

Energy	219Kcal/916kJ
Fat	10.8g
Saturated Fat	1.6g
Cholesterol	1mg
Fibre	2.4g

3 Skin the peaches or nectarines, halve and remove the stones. Mix together the almonds, yogurt, orange rind and almond essence. Spoon into the hollows of each peach half and place, cut-side down, on to the pastry rounds.

6 For the sauce, skin the peach or nectarine and halve it to remove the stone. Place the flesh in a food processor, with the orange juice, and purée it until smooth. Serve the peaches hot, with the peach sauce spooned around.

Hot Plum Batter

Other fruits can be used in place of plums, depending on the season. Canned black cherries are a convenient store-cupboard substitute.

Serves 4

450g/1lb ripe red plums,
quartered and stoned
200ml/7fl oz/scant 1 cup skimmed milk
60ml/4 tbsp skimmed milk powder
15ml/1 tbsp light muscovado (brown) sugar
5ml/1 tsp vanilla essence (extract)
75g/3oz/⅔ cup self-raising
(self-rising) flour
2 egg whites
icing (confectioners') sugar, to sprinkle

NUTRITION NOTES

Per portion

Energy	195Kcals/816kJ
Fat	0.48g
Saturated Fat	0.12g
Cholesterol	2.8mg
Fibre	2.27g

1 Preheat the oven to 220°C/425°F/
Gas 7. Lightly oil a wide, shallow ovenproof dish and add the plums.

2 Pour the milk, milk powder, sugar,
vanilla, flour and egg whites into a
food processor. Process until smooth.

3 Pour the batter over the plums. Bake
for 25–30 minutes, or until well risen
and golden. Sprinkle with icing sugar and
serve immediately.

Glazed Apricot Sponge

Puddings can be very high in saturated fat, but this one uses the minimum of oil and no eggs.

Serves 4

10ml/2 tsp golden (light corn) syrup
411g/14½oz can apricot halves in fruit juice
150g/5oz/1¼ cup self-raising
(self-rising) flour
75g/3oz/1½ cups fresh breadcrumbs
90g/3½oz/⅔ cup light muscovado
(brown) sugar
5ml/1 tsp ground cinnamon
30ml/2 tbsp sunflower oil
175ml/6fl oz/¾ cup skimmed milk

NUTRITION NOTES
Per portion

Energy	364Kcals/1530kJ
Fat	6.47g
Saturated Fat	0.89g
Cholesterol	0.88mg
Fibre	2.37g

1 Preheat the oven to 180°C/350°F/
Gas 4. Lightly oil a 900ml/1½ pint/
3¾ cup pudding bowl. Spoon in the syrup.

3 Mix the flour, breadcrumbs, sugar
and cinnamon, then beat in the oil
and milk. Spoon into the bowl and bake
for 50–55 minutes, or until firm and
golden. Turn out and serve with the
puréed fruit as a sauce.

2 Drain the apricots and reserve the
juice. Arrange about eight halves in
the bowl. Purée the rest of the apricots
with the juice and set aside.

Fruity Bread Pudding

A delicious family favourite pudding from grandmother's day, with a lighter healthier touch.

Serves 4

75g/3oz/½ cup mixed dried fruit
150ml/¼ pint/⅔ cup apple juice
115g/4oz stale brown or white
bread, diced
5ml/1 tsp mixed (apple pie) spice
1 large banana, sliced
150ml/¼ pint/⅔ cup skimmed milk
15ml/1 tbsp demerara (raw) sugar
low-fat natural (plain) yogurt, to serve

NUTRITION NOTES

Per portion
Energy	190Kcals/800kJ
Fat	0.89g
Saturated Fat	0.21g
Cholesterol	0.75mg
Fibre	1.8g

1 Preheat the oven to 200°C/400°F/ Gas 6. Place the dried fruit in a small pan with the apple juice and bring to the boil.

2 Remove the pan from the heat and stir in the bread, spice and banana. Spoon the mixture into a shallow 1.2 litre/ 2 pint/5 cup ovenproof dish and pour over the milk.

3 Sprinkle with demerara sugar and bake for 25–30 minutes, until firm and golden brown. Serve hot or cold with natural low-fat yogurt.

Cook's Tip

Different types of bread will absorb varying amounts of liquid, so you may need to adjust the amount of milk to allow for this.

Souffléed Orange Semolina

Semolina has a poor reputation as a rather dull, sloppy pudding, but cooked like this you would hardly recognise it.

1 Preheat the oven to 200°C/400°F/ Gas 6. Place the semolina in a non-stick pan with the milk and sugar. Stir over a moderate heat until thickened and smooth. Remove from the heat.

3 Whisk the egg white until stiff but not dry, then fold lightly and evenly into the mixture. Spoon into a 1 litre/ 1¾ pint/4 cup ovenproof dish and bake for 15–20 minutes, until risen and golden brown. Serve immediately.

Serves 4

50g/2oz/⅓ cup semolina
600ml/1 pint/2½ cups semi-skimmed milk
30ml/2 tbsp light muscovado (brown) sugar
1 large orange
1 egg white

NUTRITION NOTES

Per portion

Energy	158Kcals/665kJ
Fat	2.67g
Saturated Fat	1.54g
Cholesterol	10.5mg
Fibre	0.86g

2 Grate a few long shreds of orange rind from the orange and save for decoration. Finely grate the remaining rind. Cut all the peel and white pith from the orange and remove the segments. Stir the fruit into the semolina with the orange rind.

Cook's Tip
When using the rind of citrus fruit, scrub the fruit thoroughly before use, or buy unwaxed fruit.

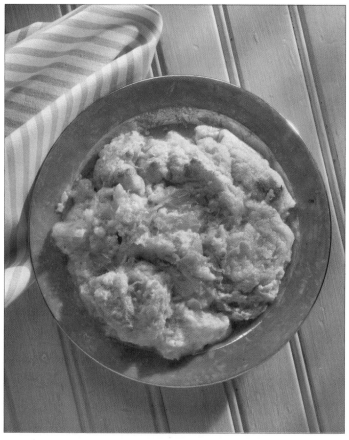

Soufflééd Rice Pudding

The fluffy egg whites in this unusually light rice pudding make the portions seem much more substantial, without adding lots of extra calories or fat.

Serves 4

50g/2oz/¼ cup short grain rice
45ml/3 tbsp clear honey
750ml/1¼ pints/3 cups semi-skimmed
(low-fat) milk
1 vanilla pod (bean) or 2.5ml/½ tsp
vanilla essence (extract)
2 egg whites
5ml/1 tsp freshly grated nutmeg

Cook's Tip

If you wish, use skimmed milk instead of semi-skimmed, but take care when it's simmering as it tends to boil over very easily with so little fat.

NUTRITION NOTES

Per portion

Energy	161Kcals/679kJ
Fat	0.9g
Saturated Fat	0.1g
Cholesterol	4mg
Fibre	0

1 Place the rice, honey and milk in a heavy or non-stick pan and bring the milk to the boil. Add the vanilla pod, if using.

2 Reduce the heat and put the lid on the pan. Leave to simmer gently for about 1–1¼ hours, stirring occasionally to prevent sticking, until most of the liquid has been absorbed.

3 Remove the vanilla pod, or if using vanilla essence, add this to the rice mixture at this stage. Preheat the oven to 220°C/425°F/Gas 7.

4 Place the egg whites in a clean, dry bowl and whisk them until they hold soft peaks.

5 Using a metal spoon or spatula, fold the egg whites evenly into the rice mixture and tip into a 1 litre/1¾ pint/4 cup ovenproof dish.

6 Sprinkle with grated nutmeg and bake for 15–20 minutes, until the pudding is well-risen and golden brown. Serve hot.

Index

Acknowledgements

The publishers would like to thank the following contributing authors: Catherine Atkinson, Jacqueline Clark, Frances Cleary, Roz Denny, Joanna Farrow, Christine France, Shirley Gill, Carole Handslip, Shezad Husain, Annie Nichols, Maggie Pannell, Katherine Richmond, Anne Sheasby, Liz Trigg and Laura Washburn. The publishers would also like to thank the following photographers: Karl Adamson, Steve Baxter, James Duncan, Michelle Garrett, Amanda Heywood, Don Last and Michael Michaels.